I'M STRONG ENOUGH
NOW GOD,
Thanks

My Journey from Trauma to Truth

KATE SHIPP

I AM STRONG ENOUGH NOW GOD, THANKS
My Journey from Trauma to Truth

ISBN: 979-8-9857929-0-4

Cover and Interior Design by
Transcendent Publishing

Although the author has made every effort to ensure that the information in this book was correct at press time, the author does not assume and hereby disclaim any liability to any party for any loss, damage, or disruption caused by errors or omissions, whether such errors or omissions result from negligence, accident, or any other cause.

I have tried to recreate events, locales and conversations from my memories of them. In order to maintain their anonymity and privacy, in some instances I have changed the names of some individuals.

The information in this book, whether provided in hardcopy or digitally, is for general information purposes, and is not a substitute for medical attention, treatment, examination, advice, treatment of existing conditions or diagnosis, and is not intended to provide a clinical diagnosis nor take the place of proper medical advice from a fully qualified medical practitioner. It does not take into account your individual health, medical, physical, or emotional situation or needs. Please consult with your own physician or healthcare specialist regarding the suggestions and recommendations made in this book. You are responsible for consulting a suitable medical professional before using any of the information or materials contained in this book or accessed through any electronic means before trying any treatment or taking any course of action that may directly or indirectly affect your health or well-being. The use of this book implies your acceptance of this disclaimer.

Printed in the United States of America.

To Connor and Makena – my children,
my whys, and my greatest joys.

To Eric, for showing me that love is safe.

TABLE OF CONTENTS

FOREWORD

by
Sunny Dawn Johnston

When Kate asked me to write the foreword for this book, I agreed immediately. A longtime student and now colleague of mine, Kate is a beautiful example of what can happen when we open up and allow the healing power of the Divine to enter our lives. When I met Kate, I could see and feel her strength and power—as well as the scared little girl within. She was a very bright light, with the dimmer switch turned on. Her lack of self-love would not allow her light to truly shine. Her body, mind, and emotions protected her beautiful Spirit in the best way it knew how. It's the way that many of us have protected ourselves from our traumas ... keeping us small.

Over the next several years, as you will read throughout this faith-filled story, Kate did the work—the hard, heavy, and necessary work to turn that dimmer switch off and let her beautiful LIGHT SHINE! The miracles and transformation that I have witnessed Kate experience over the years have inspired me as her mentor, given me hope for humanity, and offered me a safe and loving place to refer those that are in need of this very specialized support.

I'm Strong Enough Now, God. Thanks by Kate Shipp contains the wisdom of a determined woman that scraped and clawed her way from the pain of betrayal and agony to walk her extraordinary journey from Trauma to Truth. Trauma is something that you likely relate to, which unfortunately far too many people do. Truth is something so many are looking for. You will find both in the pages in front of you.

This is not a book to read for entertainment. No, this book is to be read like a manual for trauma recovery. Embedded throughout Kate's disturbing, yet relatable stories, is the Light ... and a reminder that there is always light in the darkness. Her processes, steps, and techniques will remind you of the role that faith plays in the healing journey. Her connection to God and the loving presence that manifested through magical signs and symbols will help you to find hope in your darkest days and encourage you to spread hope in your lightest ones.

Maybe you are dealing with the pain so intensely right now that you aren't sure where to turn, or what to do to feel better or shift the energy. Well, my friend, you have landed in the right place, with the right book in your hands. This is your sign that you are exactly where you need to be and that you are ready to experience LOVE and HEALING each and every day. As you read this book, you will see how God continuously guides you through the Angels, Guides, signs, and symbols. Always pay attention to the signs.

My hope is maybe, just maybe, as you read this book you will be ready to open up to forgiveness ... and through Kate's example, begin to see forgiveness as something you do to FREE yourself. You deserve FREEDOM. There will come a time when forgiveness knocks on your door, and you will have the choice to let yourself experience that gift. Please accept the gift with God's grace because you deserve the LOVE and the FREEDOM.

I cannot begin to tell you how much your life will change from the inside out when you use Kate's tools to look within, connect with that greater part of you, and love yourself through it all–the good, the not-so-good, and everything in between. Your little child within—as well as your future self—will thank you for your courage and bravery now. I'm so proud of you already. You've taken the first step ... now it's time to take the next ...

Wishing you love, light, and peace as you step into your own personal healing journey.

~ **Sunny Dawn Johnston** - Psychic Medium, Spiritual Teacher, Angel Communicator, and Author

PREFACE

I prayed to be strong; I remembered my trauma.
I prayed to be patient; I walked the road to feeling whole.
I prayed for love; I faced my shame.
I prayed for peace; I embraced my anxiety.
I prayed for joy; I swam in the deepest sadness.
I prayed to be rid of fear; I realized fear was my inner
child needing love.
I prayed for healing; I released my victim mentality.
I prayed for security; I left everything that was unstable.
I prayed for connection; I had to disconnect.
I prayed to be saved; I met Jesus.
I prayed for my life; I learned to love myself.
I prayed for confidence; I was given massive trials.
I prayed for abundance; I learned gratitude.
I prayed to see the light; I remembered I am the light.

Why am I afraid of life?

I asked myself this question after having a horrific nightmare that would become the catalyst to finally overcome "my past," though the specifics I did not completely remember. On the rare occasion I mentioned to loved ones the traumas I did remember, I would be met with words like, "Let it go."; "It happened so long ago."; "It's over. Move on."; "Get over it. You have a beautiful life now."; and "You should be happy. Look how great your life is."

I recall thinking so many times, *If it were that easy, wouldn't I be over it already? Don't you think I know that? I'm not choosing this!*

The problem was, I did not feel happy, and I did not know why.

Early in January 2016, I was sitting with God talking about the upcoming year, unfulfilled dreams, His calling for my life, and setting new goals based on that guidance. I was going through challenges in my business and my internal world. I knew it was going to be a big year of change if I wanted to break through the old patterns that were no longer serving me.

It had been many years since I'd had my children, changed careers, and started a new business, and during that time my needs had been pushed to the back burner as I struggled to manage the day-to-day responsibilities of being a working mom and a wife. I wanted to get more attuned to my body again – exercise more, eat cleaner, and take better care of myself.

I remember feeling a thunk in my stomach and pelvis when I said, "I want to be strong, God. I want to feel strong."

What I really meant was, "God, I want to feel physically fit and strong in my body," but those weren't the words I used. We've all heard the saying, "Be careful what you wish for in life," and it's true. This prayer would be received, and answered, just not in the way I thought.

It's difficult to accept the truth of a situation when you know that once you do, there is no going back. "Ignorance is bliss" may also have some truth to it, yet that kind of bliss is fleeting and only lasts until something comes along and shatters the mirror reflecting the false beliefs that life was built upon.

And, once you realize the truth of the past, you cannot suddenly, with a snap of a finger, say, "Done. I'm over it."

Believe me, I tried it for many years. It doesn't work. Talking about it doesn't make it go away either, nor does rationalizing, intellectualizing, comparing, avoiding, numbing, repressing, shoving it down. All that does is create a bigger knot that later needs to be unwound gently and over time.

The word "accept" is a word that I repulsed for so long. Acceptance meant giving up; it meant a complete letting go of my right to be angry. To accept made me a victim and I was not going to be a victim. I had this idea in my mind that to be a victim meant that you gave someone power over you, that you were out of control of your situation, and that you were not able to take care of yourself.

I was not okay with this label. I felt victims were weak and powerless – two adjectives I certainly did not want to describe me. I know, I was in complete denial and judgment.

I didn't know that accepting the label of a victim is a very necessary part of healing, especially overcoming any kind of abuse. I didn't know that accepting and validating all that had happened to me would be a critical step in the journey to remembered wholeness.

I also didn't know that my body was keeping a root wound tucked deep inside, or that just when my life was moving in the direction I had hoped for many years, it would unleash the memory and send me so far down into a well of darkness I was not sure I would find my way out.

Thousands of hours in training as a yoga therapist and energy medicine practitioner; five years into a successful private practice helping others overcome their painful pasts; and access to so many tools and teachings to help navigate trauma were still not enough to get me out of that well.

By now you might be wondering, what happened to me? What was this darkness that overtook my mind and heart? I'm not one to walk on eggshells, so let's just get it out there. These next few statements are not easy to read, so please be gentle with yourself.

(If at any time while you are reading this book you find yourself getting triggered, please go to my website,

> *https://kateshipp.com/shop/page/2/, and download the*
> *Safe Space meditation for free.)*

What traumas?

> I was sexually abused by my paternal grandfather from
> the age of two until I was six years old (I didn't con-
> sciously remember until I was thirty-five).
>
> I was raped at seventeen (although I didn't call it that
> until thirty-five years of age).
>
> I was moved by my parents across the country for
> my senior year of high school with no justifiable rea-
> son, after growing up in the same town my entire life.
> (I didn't know this had affected me so deeply, but it
> did.)
>
> At eighteen years old, I was drugged, overdosed, and left
> for dead in an epileptic coma. I was in fact pronounced
> dead twice in the emergency room, only to come back
> to life with a heightened sixth sense that I was unsure
> how to manage.
>
> Underlying all of that was a very confusing childhood
> upbringing, one enmeshed with lots of love and more
> stuff than I could ever need, as well as many unmet
> emotional needs, a codependent home environment,
> unhealthy attachment, and a sense of shame that became
> poison in my body, mind, heart, and soul.

Exhale. Yes, we all have our baggage. No family is without its dysfunction, and many have had worse experiences. Those are the statements that cause trauma to fester into disease, and shame many into never seeking to live life fully, or at all.

Life is a polarity of beauty and suffering; we would never know the capacity of either without the contrast. My life, as most of us in this world, is filled with contrasting experiences of darkness and light. The choice to walk in the light is one I make daily.

This is the story of releasing shame and grief to be able to live in joy. It is the journey of reclaiming power, safety, embodiment, dispelling fear, and embracing life again. I believe what you will find in this book is a story of Truth, of death, of faith, of hope, of tears, of reconnection, of rebirth, of miracles, of love. It is not an easy story to tell, and it may push some edges along the way. (Remember that Safe Space meditation is there for you.)

It is the magic I only thought happened in enchanting movies and fairytales, yet so much more meaningful because it is all true. This book blends humanity and spirituality in one. It opens the doors to the other side of the veil and integrates it into daily life. The magic of Love is alive and well, and will use all of life to make it visible and available if we are brave enough to say yes. Gratefully I can say, now that I am on the other side of the pain, that although at times the healing can hurt more than the wounding, in the end it is worth the consistent effort and intentional inner work to remember your wholeness.

Please be gentle and kind to yourself. These are words that play in my mind all the time now. I hope you use them as you need the reminders that you are worth the effort to live a life you love waking up to each day.

CHAPTER ONE

WHAT IS LOVE?

I grew up in a well-to-do suburb North of Chicago; think *Mean Girls* meets *Ferris Bueller*. My loud Italian/Sicilian/English/Irish/ Scottish family, though dysfunctional like most, were close and very involved in each other's lives. I am the fourth of five children – two older brothers, an older sister and a younger sister. If that doesn't give you an idea of the psychological puzzle, then the rest of this story will for sure. There is an almost thirteen-year age gap between the oldest and youngest, a span of time that often leads me to wonder how different our childhood experiences were with the same two parents.

In a large family you learn rather quickly how to fall into the mix of daily life. A corporate executive working father, a stay-at-home mom, noisy house, and lots of animals. There were rarely quiet moments, between kids screaming, animals barking and hissing, with always a friend or two around; I am still amazed that we all survived.

As a little girl I found joy in nature. I would play outside often with my older sister, running in the grass, riding bikes, playing in the sand and shore at our cottage on Lake Michigan. In fact, most of my favorite childhood memories happened on the shores of South Haven, Michigan.

There was something magical about packing up the car and making the two-and-a-half-hour drive to our cozy home on the beach. Many summers were spent making memories that last a lifetime. This was where my family became the family I know and love so much. The days were spent building sandcastles, playing in the water, and picking up glass rocks on long beach walks; nights were spent around the bonfire and watching fireworks over the water. Sand in our hair and sheets, the smell of breakfast in the morning, the sound of calming music in the evening, and the smell of a cigar or pipe when my dad joined us on the weekends.

It was here that I learned the feeling of safety and freedom. I felt carefree on the beach and in this cottage. I felt connected, loved, seen, and cherished by my family.

I love my parents and my family. I understand that my parents did the best they could with the tools they knew. I also understand that there was a lot of trauma unresolved within each of them, passed down from generation to generation, which caused behaviors and words used on us as children that were hurtful and traumatic as well.

After years of working to rewire this understanding in my nervous system, I can find peace in knowing that we can only use the tools we have and when we learn a new tool, we have a choice to use it or throw it in the pile and never pick it up again. It takes courage and boldness to learn the new tools, and even more courage and inner strength to pick that tool up daily and learn how to use it at the right time. Using a hammer when you need a stapler isn't going to work. Telling someone to calm down when they really need to run isn't going to either.

I share this because I didn't understand why my parents were the way they were until much later in life. As children, we often place our parents or caregivers on a pedestal, in the "God" role, and we look to them to know exactly what to do and keep us safe. The problem is, they are only capable of using the tools they have been given or learned on their own to provide this sense of safety to their children. At some point in time, the grown child must come to see their parents as people, and free them from the impossible expectation of giving what they did not have either. Once I began to see my parents as people, I had space to give them grace, compassion, and forgiveness.

At a young age I took on the role of people-pleaser, rescuer – "Do as you're told"; "Don't ask for too much or say too much"; and if you want to keep the peace, then just listen. What that really means is I became an expert chameleon and did not speak my mind very much, nor did I share what was happening inside of me.

I would wake up and wonder what version of my mom I was going to meet when walking out of the long hallway of bedrooms and into the living room. Some days she was smiling and happy, some days she was already pissed-off and yelling. Most days she was somewhere in between, and the slightest mishap could send her over the edge into a rage that for a young child was terrifying. Her face would change into someone I didn't recognize, and her mood would shift so fast that I had to always be on guard. Her words and her tone of voice were her weapons of choice, though I do believe she had no idea what she was doing and that it was unintentional.

Mom was always busy with something – no surprise, having five kids – and I can only imagine the internal struggles she suffered trying to take care of us. It's a lot. I get that now. As a child, without that understanding, all I knew was that she was not happy. I recall seeing her written calendar, with each day filled so full there was no space to write one more letter. I had no idea how she did it. Dinner was always cooked each night, often with some kind of homemade dessert. Her focus was always on us, even when she couldn't stand to be around us.

My favorite times with her were when we baked in the kitchen together and shopped for makeup at various department stores.

When she was centered and focused she displayed great love in affection and hugs. She had this incredible gift for floral arrangements, and turned our small basement into a creative workshop overflowing with artificial flowers, crafts, and a world where she could be. When I was down there with her, she would smile, laugh, and get lost in the beauty of creating something special.

When she was stressed, she became someone I greatly feared. She lost herself in being a mother; maybe it was to hide a deeper pain inside, maybe it was to give herself so fully to love that she forgot how to care for herself. I came to know that my mom also had a lot of unprocessed trauma, and this is why she presented in the way that she did. It was not an excuse, yet it created space for my understanding and eventual compassion.

My dad worked outside the home, and in my later adolescent years his job often took him out of town. A great provider, yet he was an emotionally unavailable man during my childhood years. Growing up in a volatile home, he had learned to shut off his emotions to survive. As an adult, he used work and financial success as a way to cope with unprocessed pain. Some of my favorite moments with my dad were when he and I went to church alone, and sometimes to the car dealership to buy or trade in a vehicle. Other times I would ask to go downtown to work with him, and several times I was allowed. I always enjoyed those days as we would take Lake Shore Drive into Chicago, and I loved the energy of the winding road through the trees, the lake lining the drive, and the busyness of the city. He was always more talkative and open one-on-one than in large groups.

At family gatherings, I would look for my dad and often found him sitting alone outside in nature. Although I didn't disturb him, I always wondered why, and as I got older I understood. He is highly sensitive too and would need to get away from all the noise and chaos to find some peace and quiet to slow down his nervous system and reset. As a child I just thought he didn't want to be around us.

When someone is suffering silently inside, it often presents as uncontrollable emotions or the inability to emotionally connect. Physical presence may be there, yet it is as if the heart is turned off and the safe space that is needed to feel loved is not available. The practices of compassion and forgiveness were critical tools and practices to help me rebuild a healthy relationship with my family.

There was one person in my life that I could always talk to and felt safe with – that was Papa, my mom's dad. He would spend intentional time with me, playing games, teaching me how to play the organ, showing me card games, going to the park, teaching me how to iron, and singing church hymns. I came to understand a connection of love and feeling important when I was spending time with him. His smile and laugh would bring joy to my heart, and although he was strict, he asked things in a way that was calm and mindful. When I think about him, my heart still smiles inside, and a little light of residual grief evokes a few tears.

Whether Papa was aware of it or not, he taught me to see the beauty in little things, to make moments count, to be present and intentional with my time, to find time to laugh and play, to work hard, to keep your brain active, to exercise regularly, to sing with your heart, and how to win at gin rummy almost always. He died when I was ten years old. His love always surrounded me, as even then I felt strongly connected to Spirit. I never doubted his spiritual presence and would use it at times when I felt afraid.

During one of my therapy sessions, after giving some insight into my family of origin, my therapist made a resounding statement that at first was very hard to understand, and over time I came to know it as truth. While the horrible experiences I had in momentary situations were awful, the root of Complex PTSD was the lack of feeling safe and secure in my childhood home each day due to emotional inconsistency.

These polarities in life – great moments of love and massive grief – created an internal environment of fear and insecurity. As an adult, it's normal not to know what life will bring. As a child, it is necessary to have a consistent environment of safety, connection, and belonging, created by one's caregivers, so that no matter what life brings, the child knows she will be loved and cared for through all of it.

I came to understand that the big "T" traumas were resting on the shaking ground of daily little "t" traumas, causing my nervous system to be a ticking time bomb waiting to explode at the slightest inkling of stress and additional responsibility. I had no space for calm, as calm was not safe.

When a nervous system is wired and developed in fear, it creates neural pathways in the brain and body that activate any time fear is not present. It is a strange way of keeping oneself safe. In a healthy nervous system, this alert would turn off, and only turn on when in danger. In the nervous system of someone developed in fear, the alert doesn't turn off. Instead it is constantly running in the background, and when something triggers it, either extreme fight/flight kicks in, or a freeze/faint response results, causing the person to shut down. Meaning, even if they wanted to fight back, to yell, to run, they can't. They are frozen.

Unfortunately, what also can happen is the instant that peacefulness, love, or safety enters the nervous system, the body/mind complex has a very hard time receiving that as "safe," because it builds its safety on an alert system of fear. This means that often people who are traumatized have a very hard time receiving love and feeling peaceful. It in fact can be extremely triggering for them.

If safety was founded upon fear, then real love is actually the most terrifying experience. When you layer in that the fear was built upon experiences where those that said they love you are the ones that caused the pain, you can now begin to understand this difficult entanglement of energy that gets activated every time there is a real experience of love.

In order to overcome this, embodied process work needs to be facilitated to help the person slowly and gently unwind the old programming, and begin to rewire the nervous system in actual safety, love, and healthy connection. This takes time, patience, and a lot of self-compassion.

All of this was what was happening inside of me every single day. The love from my husband, Eric, and my children, was triggering me. It is so painful to imagine that Love can be triggering, and yet it is true.

I had a belief running in my programming that said, "People who love you, hurt you. In order to love someone, you have to hurt them." I realized this belief was in my unconscious mind during a trauma therapy session in 2017.

I know. Terribly sad. So painful, and yet, that was the belief I adopted to make sense of very confusing messaging and experiences from a young toddler through my teenage years, finally coming to a head at thirty-five years old.

As a parent now myself, I can empathize with my parents, and I understand how even with the best of intentions, and the goodness of love inside us, unconscious pain has a way of sneaking up and out at the most inappropriate times. While the intent is not to cause another harm, the devastation and fear that it creates for a child can cause lifelong suffering unless that person takes the time to go within and remedy the unmet need.

I recall being so thankful for the memories of what real love is, and able to access that at times when my fear would overcome me. I had no idea that belief was active in my brain and body until one therapy session where a part of me revealed this unbearable pain.

During an EMDR session[1], my therapist pointed out that my left shoulder was tense and jammed up into my left ear. The website, www.emdr.com, defines EMDR (Eye Movement Desensitization and Reprocessing) as a psychotherapy that enables people to heal from the symptoms and emotional distress resulting from disturbing life experiences.[1] My therapist used a body-centered approach, meaning the therapeutic work was focused on what was also happening in my body, as well as my mind.

She asked me to notice this imbalance in my shoulders. I was able to connect to a nine-year-old part of myself that always felt responsible for how others felt. This part was only wanting to be loved and feel loved. She would do everything she could to make someone love her, and please others. This is where that "fawning" response of the nervous system comes into awareness. While many are familiar with the fight/flight and freeze/faint responses, fawning is a more recent and lesser-known term for a self-protective response. I first learned of this through studying Pete Walker's book, *Complex PTSD: From Surviving to Thriving*.[2]

The fawning response is where a person, in my case as a young child, adapts to be what others expect or want them to be so attention and love can be received. This often develops into a codependency trait, and combines with shame to form a personal belief system that, "I am only loveable if... and I am only worthy of love when..." The ends of those statements are based upon the action of the child in relation to meeting the demands of the adult or other person. For example, I had a belief that I was only worthy of love if I did what was asked of me and met expectations of those in authority over me.

This nine-year-old part of me was desperately seeking love. In this EMDR I was able to learn that she felt so scared of being loved because that often meant she would be hurt. In unraveling this pain, I came to realize that this was the part of me that would withhold love, and would run from it, as a way to protect from being hurt.

In order to overcome this deeply wired, unhealthy pattern, and open my heart to receiving love, I needed to focus on giving myself consistency, safety, security, and healthy emotional processing.

I had to learn to titrate love experiences in small, digestible doses, then slowly increase the dose a little at a time. My nervous system had to learn that love is safe, and that I am worthy of feeling loved. Knowing you are loved and feeling loved are two very different experiences. When there is developmental childhood trauma mixed with loving experiences, the child grows to doubt love, and may believe that their parents love them yet don't feel that love due to the experiences when love was conditional.

Learning how to love, what love is, how to receive love, and how to feel loved are all steps to healing. By gently receiving loving experiences, naming them and noticing the sensational manifestations of love in my body, then I was finally able to feel loved. Once I could feel love, then I could discern if situations were safe or unsafe. I could make choices that aligned with love, allowing for a more joyful daily life.

While I could not change how my parents treated me as a child, I could control whether I allowed that to cause suffering any longer. As I began to heal, I birthed a deep compassion and grace to the suffering that can come from the wounding of the unresolved past. It was not my fault that my parents were the way that they were when I was young. Their past pain dripped onto me, and I did what I needed to do to get through those very hard moments. They provided for me and loved me in the best ways they knew how. They gave me what they were capable of giving, and although it was not completely what I needed, it was my choice to do the work to process the unmet needs, and reprogram my heart for new understanding and healthy living.

C H A P T E R   T W O

COPING SKILLS

I feel things deeply. I always have. I guess I just didn't understand any of that until I was well into my mid-twenties and trying to make sense of why I would experience life very differently than many of the people around me.

I came to understand that I have the gifts of empathy, seeing, and hearing. I would learn that these are intuitive gifts given to us by God, and we each have them all, yet some are more heightened than others. I also came to understand that when you experience trauma at a young age, these senses become more acute to protect you outwardly, by helping you sense things that others are not as open to receiving.

It is like having octopus arms out all around you, picking up the unseen energies and sending messages back into your heart to tell your gut what is happening so it can send a signal to your brain to react. This incredible ability becomes a problem when your nervous system develops around fear and the wiring of your brain starts to connect on the signals that life is not safe. Then it is difficult to discern whether the messages being sent to the body are born truly of fear or of trauma, talking and creating a world inside based on the fears of the outside.

I began to believe that the only way to survive this kind of internal chaos is to become what the world needs you to be. Granted, I did not have this language as a child, and I would not come to understand any of this until I was thirty-five years old. It is the intelligence of our heart that knows what we need to do in order to make it through the pain. When life becomes safe enough, the heart begins to unwind the pain, and it will then reveal the wounding so it can feel whole again.

This unwinding is often referred to as "the dark night of the soul," a term originally coined by Spanish mystic and poet St. John of the Cross. I agree with that message and meaning. I also believe it could be called the "illumination of the light in the heart" as when someone goes through horrific experiences in their life, they turn out their light internally to protect it from being hurt even more.

I believe that the dark night of the soul is the sacred journey inward to the deepest layers of the wounding of the heart to reclaim the pieces of you that fragmented during the traumas and guide them back home. The illumination of the light in the heart is to breathe life back into the part of you untouched by the suffering of this world and allow that light to guide you into remembering your wholeness. It is this light that can hold all the pain, all the sadness, all the fear, all the anger, while at the same time holding all the joy, all the love, all the peace. It is the entire ocean within you, waiting for the waves frozen in time to melt into love.

There are many coping skills that one learns during times of suffering and when young, most of these skills are learned by watching what others do to manage their own stress and pain.

When I was in my younger and adolescent years, I chose to use coping skills like blending in, being silent, screaming, and slamming doors. When those didn't work, I started exercising and drinking too much in high school and early college; then after the overdose, I chose to avoid all drugs except alcohol and instead used work and school as a means to numb the deep pain and sadness fighting to be heard and seen inside. It was much more admirable and acceptable to work hard and be successful. People praised those traits even if they were just a mask for pain.

When I was eight years old I was invited to watch a family friend ride horses for the day at a local stable. It was instant love for me. Something about the magic of a horse that attracted my heart. I asked my parents if I could start to ride and take lessons.

Horses became a safe haven for my heart. I would ride as often as I could for as long as I was allowed. I even had the stable van come pick me up from school to take me straight to the barn for a few hours a couple days a week. When I was on a horse I felt safe, I felt seen by my instructors, I felt like I was important and that I mattered. No, I did not have those words, though I do recall saying many times how even though these animals are twelve hundred pounds and could hurt me very easily, I did not fear them. The only fear I had was of them biting me, which actually did happen many times. That never stopped me from loving them.

When I was riding, I felt free. The wind on my face, in my hair, the rhythm of the hoofbeats beneath me, the strength and stability of an animal moving me through time – it is still one of my favorite pastimes, and I still have a longing in my heart to own my own horse. It will be a gift to my inner child.

I started riding just a couple years after the sexual abuse by my paternal grandfather ended. I hadn't told anyone about the abuse, and wouldn't until I was thirty-five. He had threatened me, and I was terrified of him. Horses became my therapy, not that I realized it at that young age. All I knew was I felt safe and free and loved by these creatures. That is what I needed - safety and love. Primal needs are so often unmet by those who say they love us the most.

A moment that stands out to me is when I was in junior high and riding at a smaller stable where I could learn from Dan, a well-known trainer in the area. He was trying to help me learn to trust myself and work through my fears through riding. At this point I was a jumper and loved the feeling of flying through the air on the back of my favorite horse, Marco Polo.

When I arrived at the stable that day, Dan said, "Go get Marco Polo, but don't saddle or bridle him. You will be riding bareback and without reins today."

I didn't really think twice about it, as he had done this before. He was teaching me to feel the horse, to connect our energies and read each other without the use of the saddle and reins. Horses naturally do this, attuning to our energy without us knowing. In the past we did arena work like this, changing gaits and making different patterns around the ring using only my legs and breath. It was an energetic way of asking for what I need without using words. These were my first lessons in energy, but I didn't know it at that time.

When I brought Marco Polo to the arena that day, there was only one other rider – a younger girl – and another trainer. My mom stayed to watch that day, a rare occurrence.

Dan had me come to the center of the arena, gave me a leg up onto my horse, and then just looked at me.

"You are going to jump today. Without a saddle and without reins."

I think my eyes popped out of their sockets. "What?"

"You heard me."

Dan was not a man who liked to repeat himself.

"I'm not ready for that. I can't do that. How is that even possible?"

"You can and you will. It is time you start to trust yourself and your horse more."

We started that lesson just riding around the arena. My heart was pounding out of my chest. He had me doing simple turns, lead changes, trotting, cantering, finding my center and balance on Marco Polo's back. I talked with my horse the entire time, telling him what was going to happen, how I was feeling, and just praying that I did not fall off over the jumps.

Dan was setting up the jumps in the arena. I'd thought they would be a foot, maybe two feet high, at most. Nope. I am not sure how high they were, but my guess is that they were well over three feet, and there were two of them, one after another, with one more on the other side of the arena.

After telling me to come to the center, Dan said, "Here is how this is going to go. You will pick up a canter around on this lead, then make your way to approach these two jumps. You will fix your gaze on the other side of each jump, allowing your legs to support you, keeping your stomach strong, and your breath moving. If you stop breathing, he will stop moving. If you let off your legs, he will stop. He is listening to your body and to your breathing. He needs you as much as you need him. You are a team. Your hands will hold his mane gently as support. No pulling. His gaze will follow yours. You two will become one. You can do this. You will do this. I believe in you. After you clear these two jumps, you will keep going to the end, turn, change leads, and approach the final jump, repeating just what I said. Trust him. He trusts you. Trust yourself, Kate. Have some faith and make it happen."

I exhaled and patted Marco Polo on the right side of his neck. *He trusts me,* I thought. *And I do trust him.* I just didn't trust myself much. I don't remember if my mom was watching. I had tunnel vision at this point. All I heard was my heartbeat, my horse's breath, his hooves, and Dan's voice. Everything else went silent. I recall Dan asking that the other girl stop her lesson for a few minutes so there would be no other distractions for me or for my horse. I admit that scared me a bit. Was this a normal thing he did?

I quickly glanced at the other trainer. She smiled at me and nodded her head. She must have been used to this from Dan. I hugged my horse with my legs and off we went. I cantered him a few times around the arena, linking our movement and breath. I whispered to him about what we were going to do. Dan's words played on repeat in my mind, "Trust yourself, Kate. Have some faith and make it happen."

I turned to the left to make our way down the length of the arena heading towards the first two jumps, my gaze focused on the other side of them. There was about one stride worth of space between the first two, which meant we would land the first jump, take one stride, make the second jump, and then do a fairly quick turn, change leads, take a few more strides, and then clear the third jump.

I followed Dan's instruction to the letter, hugging in with my legs, using my core and my thighs to lift my seat off his back as I gently held his mane and leaned forward. When I noticed I had stopped breathing I started again. "Two more lengths," I heard Dan say, "You got this! Trust yourself."

We lifted off, flying through the air, just me and my horse, nothing and no one else. We landed, one stride and up and over again, our breath linked as one, we landed, made the turn, changed leads, three lengths, and the final jump. I could feel the excitement in my blood and veins. Adrenaline pumping through me. Marco Polo's breath came heavier and faster, my body moving in sync with his gaits. I hugged in tighter, lifted and leaned in, took a breath and on the exhale up we went over and cleared the jump. We landed clean, and cantered off to the end of the arena. Tears flowed from my eyes and Dan was screaming and cheering. The other trainer was clapping for me and the little girl on her horse was squealing in delight and awe.

I brought my horse to the center of the arena, quickly wiped my tears, and smiled at Dan.

"You did it!" he exclaimed, "YOU did it! Great job. You just gotta believe in yourself. And in your horse. You are capable of so much more. You two have a great bond. It's special. Way to go! You will remember this for a long time."

I leaned forward and gave Marco Polo a huge hug. I walked him out, cooling him off, my heart beaming and smiling in great joy. I was so proud of myself. Then the small pain of grief struck my heart. "No one will understand," my inner voice said quietly. "I don't have anyone I can really share this with." I felt the joy fade and that shadow of sadness overtake my heart once again. I don't remember if my mom said anything about it.

I remember going home that day so excited for what I had accomplished and yet so sad that I could not share this with my family. No one would care – at least that's what I felt. I wished I could just stay at the barn. I felt safe there.

Riding would take me through early junior high, and even helped me heal from the death of my Papa. Losing him devastated my eleven-year-old heart, and horses were my sanctuary from the surges of anger and sadness that would often overcome me in the late evening hours of each day. A ride on my horse would clear the pain and open up the well of joy to contain a few drops again.

As I entered seventh grade, I became more involved with playing sports and socializing. Horseback riding wasn't cool anymore in the eyes of my friends, and in order to keep growing I would have had to start doing larger shows, which meant more money and training. That scared me and I didn't want to be a financial burden on my parents. My dad was traveling a lot more, my oldest brother was in college, and the other would soon be leaving as well. Mom was less happy and more stressed as our schedules got busier and more fell on her plate. I told my parents I would quit riding, that I didn't want to do it anymore, which was a lie but kept things peaceful and easier for them. I set this grief deep into my heart and wouldn't process it for many years. I settled for volleyball and basketball, and though I was good at both neither fed my heart and soul.

As the years went on, I came to understand that beauty and fitting in were more important than being smart and kind. Though I still did very well in school, I began to carve my character and physical form into society's standards of what makes a woman attractive. I was starving for attention and belonging, not knowing who I was nor who I wanted to be. All I wanted was to feel loved, but couldn't because of a large wall in my heart due to the pains from years past. Please remember that I had blocked out the memory of sexual abuse. Sure, I am positive that somewhere in my being I had memories of it and, as you will soon learn, it was definitely holding in my subconscious mind.

Every time I saw my grandfather my shoulders would collapse around my heart, I would feel dizzy, and my legs would feel like Jell-o. I developed stomach pains after eating anything. Numerous medical tests found nothing wrong, yet the pain continued.

I also had headaches that felt like stabbing in the back of my head and a halo around my eyes. No one mentioned anxiety or unprocessed trauma; no one noticed that these symptoms that had followed me my entire life were signs of dissociation and PTSD. I just thought it was normal to feel this way.

I learned to numb the pain and not pay attention to it. For the most part I didn't eat much, but when I did and it hurt, I would make myself throw up. I never self-labeled with an eating disorder, however, I was probably close to it.

I was unaware that these were all ways my body was trying to tell me that something was wrong mentally and emotionally, manifesting through my body as imbalances and dis-ease.

I moved through my teenage years with great grades, good friendships, many bad decisions, and a couple of other traumatic experiences. I stayed in that energy of being what others wanted me to be, never establishing a healthy relationship with myself, with my body, or with the truth of who I am – which is probably not all that uncommon. All the while, I felt like I was floating away in this world, sometimes unintentionally landing into emotion, and sometimes just moving through the motions without making true connection and healthy bonding.

Fast forward to a college degree, a marriage to a wonderful man very young, the purchase of a house, the attainment of a good job, and the birthing of two beautiful children. Eight years after completing my bachelor's degree I went back to school to be a yoga therapist and energy medicine practitioner; I owned a yoga studio, worked harder than ever before to build a successful private practice, helping many clients and students overcome trauma, PTSD, anxiety, depression, chronic pain, physical illness, and more.

I thought the little bit of healing work I had done over a few years was enough to heal my psyche from the intense, unfortunate happenings that had left my inner world in a constant state of frozen or ready-to-run at the sound of a door slamming shut. However, while my mind may have moved forward and learned new skills and acquired new tools, my body was still living in the trauma as if it was always happening. No amount of coping was enough to clear the energy out of my body. No amount of repressing was going to change what happened. No amount of numbing, work, education, or filling up with stuff was going to process out the pain that was making it hard to show up for my family and for myself each day.

The only way out is through, and by through I mean taking a backpack full of all your strongest tools, of all different sizes (most of which will not work), and acquiring an entire new set along the way. I mean taking a bright flashlight - hoping it works and that you remember to use it – along with some nourishment, a connection to a clear, rational voice, and going underground into the depths of unknown darkness to reclaim the pieces of you that were left behind for so many years.

CHAPTER THREE

THE DIAGNOSIS

When I was diagnosed with complex PTSD (CPTSD) in 2016, also known as developmental trauma, I was deeply surprised. In my mind, I was the one helping those heal from PTSD, not the one living with it, let alone for almost thirty years. While PTSD is usually related to a one-time or series of traumatic events in a short period of time, most often referred as everything was different after that, complex PTSD results from a series of traumatic events that repeatedly occurred over a long period or from things never being safe and okay, leading to a complexity of imbalances. As mentioned previously, my developmental trauma was indeed compounded and exacerbated by other traumatic events throughout my life. If you skipped the preface, I recommend going back to read about these events. I will give more details on them throughout the book, as integrating each experience was an important process in reclaiming the pieces of me that had been left behind.

Have you ever read the children's book, *Going on a Bear Hunt* by Michael Rosen? If not, I recommend checking it out as it parallels healing from CPTSD. It is the story of a family going to hunt a bear, which to me symbolizes hunting down their greatest fear. On their journey they come across many different landscapes and obstacles on their path. They learn quickly that they "can't go under it, they can't go over it, they have to go through it."

I remember when my kids were little, I would read this book to them. We would make silly noises to give voice to the many different ways the family had to conquer their obstacles to get closer to their goal of finding the bear. My kids would get so nervous when we came to the part when the characters see the bear in the cave! Screaming, they run the way they had come, back through all the obstacles they had conquered, this time with the bear on their heels. When they finally make it home safely, the bear stares inside for a while then walks away with its head down.

When I think about that book now, I believe the family knew that in order to move forward to overcome their fear, they first needed to find it. They quickly learned they had to go through the obstacles to reach their goal. Once they found the fear, they allowed the fear to take them over instead of remembering why they started the journey in the first place.

The bear (fear) simply wanted to be a part of the family, and it chased them back home because they had allowed it to get the best of them, instead of facing it and listening to what it had to say, embracing the fear, and learning how it too has gifts waiting to be discovered and loved.

I believe our human journey is much the same. We know at some point that to get to the other side of fear we need to go through the pain, meet the fear, and be with it to learn that it is really just a part of us, seeking our compassion and love. And like the family in the story, we often meet the fear and run, never knowing the beauty that comes from understanding and welcoming what it represents.

I'm forty now, ten years into a deep healing journey to joy. I say "deep healing" because I do believe that when I was twelve years old and my family welcomed a shamanic healer into our lives, I started learning more about the mind/body/heart/soul connection than I realized in my younger years. I'll share more about that in another chapter.

When I was twenty-six, Eric gave me a gift certificate to a yoga studio to find a hobby and better manage the stress of being a young mom. I was experiencing postpartum depression but didn't know it. I just thought I was struggling with managing being a new mother, a wife, and working full-time.

My first yoga class shifted something in my heart and body. After studying and understanding so much about energy, chakras, and spirit, I was still missing the connection and integration of it all into my body. This first yoga class would be the catalyst that eventually helped me find myself again and recover from the daily effects of CPTSD.

I was someone who loved to exercise; as shared earlier, it became a way of dealing with the stress and anger I felt often throughout my teenage years. Going to the gym to sweat it out, lifting weights to prove I was strong, were daily habits. I did not think yoga would be hard. I was wrong. The postures worked muscles I didn't know I had. The mindful breathing was difficult yet reminded me of breathing while horseback riding. Since I was a total type-A competitor, I thought the more I pushed myself, the better yoga student I would be; however, as my yoga teacher said, "I was practicing exercise and insanity, not yoga."

I took classes daily, immersing myself in this practice that for some reason just felt good. I would leave class feeling lighter, stronger, and more flexible. My chest was not as tight and my stomach did not hurt anymore. I was better able to handle the daily stresses that being a mom brings.

I recall in one class, after much shaking and panting to force my hunched-over body into triangle pose, the teacher approached me and gently asked, "Where are you trying to get into? Please come down to child's pose and breathe. You are going to hurt yourself."

Reluctantly, I listened. As soon as I followed her instructions, I was hit by a wave of peace and a softening in my mind. *What?!* I remember thinking, *I can rest? I'm receiving permission to rest, relax, and breathe?* At that moment, I knew the practice of yoga was going to change my life.

In the other types of exercise I did, the harder you push, the better the results. Or so I thought. I never once considered that I was pushing too hard. My nervous system didn't know how to relax. In fact, it would resist the idea and feeling. When relaxation did kick in, cortisol would push through it. I realized it did not feel safe for me to relax.

I'd been blessed with an upbringing that exposed me to religion, shamanic practices, meditation, and the energy body; however, these concepts were so esoteric and "woo-woo" that I did not grasp their connection to day-to-day life. It all felt "out there," and nothing helped me feel "in here" except exercise. The constant pushing of my body to the point of deep physical feeling helped me to feel alive. It was also pushing my adrenals into burnout.

I credit the practice of yoga with helping me recover from the depression I experienced after the birth of my son. While I didn't understand what was happening to me internally, because I had not yet learned the philosophy of yoga, I knew that I was shifting on my ability to handle the external.

I remember being asked if I had ever cried in yoga. I guess it was "a thing," but I had not experienced it; in fact, I couldn't even imagine crying in front of people I didn't know. Then it happened. I was lying in savasana (or "corpse" pose), which is the last pose of the yoga practice and signifies the death of the practice as well as the death of who you were in the practice and of the old energy and unhealthy ways of being – when I felt a stirring in my heart. It was that same feeling from childhood of sadness, of wanting to get up and move my body as a distraction from the pain.

Instead of getting up and running out of class, I took a long exhale. I felt a crack in my heart as tears started streaming down my cheeks. It was as if someone had finally chipped deep enough into my heart wall that the well of hurt stored inside began to leak out from my eyes.

I don't remember what the class was about or what the teacher said. All I knew was that it was the first time I can recall feeling safe to cry in a room full of strangers. Lying on my back, my body still but not frozen in fear, each tear ran its course out of my eyes and onto the mat that supported me on the earth. I had built up very strong walls, and yoga had finally succeeded in breaking them down to reveal a tiny sliver of the light within my heart.

Yoga became a practice of connection to my spirit, and a way of rebuilding a relationship to my body. I practiced at least four or five days a week and sought the solace of moving my body with my breath.

I wanted to attend yoga teacher training in 2008 but found out I was pregnant with my second child. This was a blessing as we were trying to conceive. I just didn't expect it to happen suddenly. It had taken over a year to conceive the first time.

I had also struggled throughout that pregnancy: my body went into early labor at thirty weeks and I was put on bed rest for the remainder of the pregnancy. Just six weeks later I delivered, thankfully a healthy boy, who we named Connor. However, the medication I was given during bed rest caused mental imbalances and physical distress to the point where I had to be taken off it. I was, and still am, sensitive to many western medications.

Due to my past traumas, I had a very hard time connecting to my son. I didn't experience that joyful bliss that they talk about in all the pregnancy books. I didn't have the beautiful bonding experience. I struggled to breastfeed as the medication dried up my milk, and at just ten days old my child ended up in the hospital for over a week with a UTI. The nurses were unkind to me about not exclusively breastfeeding, only exasperating the shame I already felt as a new mom.

All of this led me into a depression that I didn't understand, and at that time couldn't name. I just knew that I so desperately wanted to connect with my son. Yoga helped me to build that connection.

When I found out I was pregnant with my daughter Makena, I was so excited to use yoga as a way of healthier connection to my body and to the growing baby inside me. Unfortunately my body was not comfortable being pregnant. Even with the renewed connection with myself, I was struggling internally with a lot of irrational anger that would emerge out of nowhere at my son and Eric. My husband had always said that I changed once I had my son. I felt that too, but it would be ten years before I came to know why.

My psychiatrist in 2016-2017 helped me to understand. He said that had it not been so many years since I had a child, he would consider a diagnosis of postpartum depression due to CPTSD. It is common for a woman's body to begin to activate unprocessed traumas when she is growing a child in her womb. I personally believe this is to help prevent the trauma from passing to the baby, however, without the right care, and awareness of what is happening, it can lead to further mental/emotional imbalance for the mother during and after the pregnancy.

Halfway through the pregnancy with our daughter, my husband and I decided we needed to foreclose on our home. The housing market was crashing and we were very upside down on our purchase price. Though our lawyer had recommended the foreclosure, I was grief-stricken about having to walk away from a home we'd thought we would live in for many years. Worse yet, we were unsure of where we were going to go.

We lived in Peoria, Arizona, and I was working remotely for a dermatology practice out of Chicago. My job required that I travel there every six weeks for one week at a time. My husband was working full-time, and while I was away he was caring for our two-year-old son on his own. The stress caused me to experience another early labor, this time at twenty-four weeks.

I convinced my doctors to let me stay out of bedrest on the promise that I would not overdo it, but I was devastated when they told me I had to stop practicing yoga. I promised myself that day that I would still breathe and meditate as a way of connecting to my body instead of further rejecting it for not doing what I wanted it to do during the pregnancy. Little did I know that I was actually practicing more yoga at this time internally than ever before. My yoga became breathing each day, going on walks, and being outside with my son, all while trying to calm down, shut out the fear and focus on being well.

My husband and I were not faring well in our marriage, and doing our best to make it through for our children. Eric was cycling through bouts of depression and living in a lot of shame from his own unprocessed pain. Our energy went into our son, and in making plans to find a new place to live. We were blessed that my in-laws offered us a rental home before the foreclosure happened, providing much-needed relief-a Divine gift, indeed.

I successfully held the pregnancy to thirty-eight weeks, delivered in mid-May, and thankfully did not experience the depression afterward that I had with my son. I attribute this to my yoga practice, help from our shaman, certain herbs that help balance hormones postpartum, and a healthier relationship with my body.

Two months later, in July 2009, I started back to my yoga practice. I was so happy to be on my mat, moving my body with my breath, and returning to that sense of peace that always came during savasana. I wish I could say that the anger went away and all was well, but if that were the case I would not be writing this book, nor would I have learned so much about how our humanness craves the love of our spirit.

As my kids grew, my anger grew too. I would go from being happy to angry, from being angry to sad, from sad to happy – a triangle that at any moment could turn. I felt totally out of control of the experience. I was repeating patterns that I experienced as a child and I hated myself for it.

The only calm I found was on my yoga mat, and when I was working. Eric and I were still not doing well as a couple, and now our attention was needed to be on our growing family and their well-being. I started traveling again in late summer of 2009, which meant Eric now had to care for an infant and a toddler for at least six days at a time. My income was needed to support our family, but I also welcomed the few days away, when I had to be responsible only for myself.

My kids went to daycare each day, and at night we would come together as a family, although I often felt not present nor able to be present. I was tired, stressed, and overwhelmed with packing; I also had no sense of who I was anymore.

Our move into the rental home that November created a huge shift and a rebirth of sorts, as we got out of a huge mortgage and into a more manageable financial situation. Eric and I felt some instant relief in making this change. Things started looking up and we settled into being a family together. Mind you, we had many happy moments in those early years, however, they were always veiled by this layer of shame that we both were living under as we tried to prove our worth through our successes. Neither of us was aware of this for another few years. Our bond was love coupled with underlying trauma and shame, with each of us living out the unworthiness stories in our minds.

I continued practicing yoga five days a week and was finding some stabilization in my mind, yet my heart continued to carry this pain. It would come out in the unhealthiest ways – yelling at my kids (mostly my son, who was in his "terrible threes") for no reason, when sounds were too loud, when they wanted my attention but I was needing to focus on something else, when he would have an accident in his underwear. I was unkind and unsure how to be any different in those moments when my emotions took over my mouth.

There were also many beautiful moments of playing at the park, going on walks, scooter rides, playing together in the backyard, dancing, singing, learning together. It was either all good or I was a mess. There was very little grey space. I was becoming the Jekyll- and-Hyde mother, the emotionally unavailable parent, and while I deeply wanted to connect, I felt triggered whenever I felt so loved. I would have an angry outburst and then not understand what happened and feel deep regret for yelling, a layer of shame settling in over me again.

Both children were in daycare at an in-home and did well there. My traveling continued through most of 2010, until one fall evening before I was to leave on yet another trip. "Mommy," my son said, "how come when Joey wakes up in the morning, his mommy is always there and sometimes when I wake up, you are not home?"

My heart sank. I remembered this feeling all too well, as my dad also traveled a lot when I was a child. I would often wake up and he would be gone, having been picked up hours before by a limo that would take him to the airport. I had promised myself that I would not be a traveling parent, at least not when my kids were young, yet there I was, the walking embodiment of my own upbringing – inconsistent, unregulated, unpredictable. Unprocessed trauma repeats itself generationally until one person chooses to end it. That night, as I put my son to sleep, I held him tightly in my arms and promised that I would find a way to make money without having to leave every six weeks.

My next trip, in December 2010, would be my last. God listens, and this time He gave me what I wanted. I was let go from that position in February of 2011, which was partly my choice, part the company wanting someone in-house to attend to marketing. Fear of financial concerns overwhelmed me, yet I knew this was the best thing for me and my family's well-being.

I was thirty years old, married to a great man, mother to two incredible little humans. I was also, since leaving my previous position, working for a media recruiting company from home and learning about my passion for yoga. Yet I was so unhappy; I felt very unsettled in my heart and soul. Never one to settle, I chose to pivot and change my life. I made the huge decision to finally take yoga teacher training – one of my goals for years.

If you had told me that choosing this path was going to bring me through the darkest night of my soul, I most likely would have said one of two things, "Bring it!" or "I'm out." This decision would become the start of the unraveling of my world, and the beginning of the life God intended for me to live. This was the beginning of taking my power back, and writing a new story for my own life and for my family.

CHAPTER FOUR

ACCEPTANCE

The yogic teachings refer to making an internal paradigm change as the "shift from thinking and doing to feeling and being."[3] When this shift occurs, one moves from reaction to response, from stress-based living to present-moment awareness. This to me is a key part of acceptance. In order to begin to heal, one must accept that "it is what it is." I really used to hate that phrase. It was like nails on a chalkboard to my heart, so if hearing that causes chills up your spine, hang with me for a bit.

What it really means is to shift from resistance into acceptance. To understand that in order to move forward, you must move through it. On a physiological level, it means that your nervous system shifts out of a fight-or-flight stress response into a balanced, neutral state of being. When we resist what is, we are inducing a stress response in the body.

Sometimes the stress response goes into hypervigilance, causing anxiety, worry, overwhelm, maybe even panic. The tendency is to kick into control mode and try to do something to fix or resolve the situation. On the opposite side of the spectrum you have the faint-or-freeze response of the nervous system, where you may find yourself actually locked in place. You can't make a decision; you feel stuck, in shock, shame, unable to move physically or change your perception mentally.

When there is a history of trauma, the primal immobilized reaction often kicks in, and the shut-down response takes over. This is why many trauma survivors are upset that they didn't fight back or why they couldn't find the strength to run. Often the emotional state moves into depression and a sense of despair overcomes your being. An internal nagging question plays on repeat: "Will this pain ever end?"

While I won't go into an entire lecture on the nervous system and PolyVagal theory by Dr. Stephen Porges,[4] I will share that the vagus nerve, or tenth cranial nerve, has been studied significantly regarding its response to trauma, and the intelligence of the autonomic nervous system in responding to threats based upon our programming. This means that when there is unprocessed trauma, the program running the show at any sign or perception of danger *is* the trauma. The rational mind goes offline, and the emotional brain takes the driver's seat.

The vagus nerve is responsible for sending the signals from major organs up an information highway into the brain, with fewer signals then being sent back into the body. This further explains how the body must be used in therapy to overcome trauma.

"Neuroception" a term coined by Porges, is the perception of the nervous system to any situation or environment. While the situation may be safe, if the nervous system perceives anything that mimics or feels like a threat similar to something from the past that did not end well, the vagus nerve sends those signals to the brain, causing the amygdala (a small area that regulates emotions) to go into overdrive. This is often when the symptoms of PTSD begin to present in the person as emotional or physical flashbacks. Neither the extreme fight/flight nor faint/freeze response is helpful when it comes to healing from PTSD, yet each plays a very important role in protecting you from the trauma and for survival. Your body did exactly what it was supposed to do at the time of the trauma to help you live through the experience. The inability to fight or run, the shutdown response that feels so scary and frustrating at the time, and the dissociation and out-of-body-like experience, are all internal acts of being your own savior in that terrifying moment.

If the emotional brain had not hijacked the rational mind, the reaction and response would have moved through you, like water moves down a river. However, if the experience was too big or intense for your nervous system to process at that time – be it due to your age, the extremity of the situation, or because it was just too much – it becomes like a dam was put up in the river, and the water that was supposed to flow through is now stuck. Most likely, you don't know that there is a dam, and you don't know how to move or remove it.

Here is a metaphor for what happens in your nervous system.

We are made of mostly water. Experiences are meant to move through us like water.

When you get triggered, there is a block in how your energy is moving through you.

Spiritual energy (life) and Somatic (body-based) energy (survival) are in a battle. They work against each other instead of together. This becomes an overactive nervous system response.

The hope is that we can learn how to bring regulation into the nervous system by bringing the clear mind online, while keeping presence in the feeling body, meaning experiencing the stress as sensation in the body, and learning how to be with that experience in a new way. This is done through conscious breathing.

Your body then becomes the vehicle of transformation and healing instead of something you numb and avoid.

If you can slow down enough to notice where the trigger is showing up as a physical response – a sinking stomach, tight fists, curled-up toes, clenching jaw, armored heart, squeezed buttocks, rounded shoulders, or collapsed chest – you can begin to use the body to release the trigger.

Think of a clogged drain in the bathtub. Eventually no water can get down. It keeps backing up. If you don't turn the water off and remove the clog, the bathtub overflows, and you have a flood on your hands.

Your nervous system does the same thing. Fight or flight becomes the unhealthy, static norm of your nervous system or faint/freeze overrides to try and help you survive by shutting down the body's ability to fight back.

You must begin to slowly remove the clogged energy so vital life can flow through you again. If you remove the clog too quickly, too much energy moves too fast and you may end up in a deep release. You must move your body and breathe into it to let the energy move through you gently and slowly.

Sometimes, the trauma was so much, so pervasive, that the water freezes altogether. Like ice in the water pipe, this shock response gets stuck inside your system and causes a complete disconnect from that which brings life.

If that is the case, you must let the ice begin to melt so it can start flowing. Again, slow, deep breathing acts as a gentle heater inside; so does safety, trust, rapport, empathy, connection, and love. Once there is melt-off, the water slowly starts to drain.

As you learn to titrate, a little bit of processing and releasing at a time, you build your container to be stronger and more resilient. Think about it this way: if you have two cups of water and you put those two cups in a two-cup container, it is full; it may even overflow. If you have a container that can hold eight cups, those two cups only take up a fourth of the container. The two cups of water do not change. What changes is the container's capacity.

Another way of saying this is that you need to learn how to hold more energy. The more energy you can hold, the less affected you are by stress.

As you increase your capacity for holding more energy, you increase resiliency.

As you build your resiliency, the trigger no longer affects you as it used to, and eventually it no longer has a hold on you in any way.

You begin to see it from a new perspective. You begin to love it back into wholeness. You begin to understand that all this time it was a screaming child inside waiting for you to hold it with compassion and grace.

You embody the presence of Divine Grace in all parts of you. Every aspect of the self integrates as part of the whole.

The once-frozen ice or tsunami of water is soothed back into an ocean of love.

This is healing. This is recovery. This is freedom.

Now, "it is what it is" means only that "it happened." That's it. It happened. Once I started to accept this, I began to understand that acceptance is a gradual process that opens the window to release stuck emotional energy, and that just because it happened does not mean you are a bad person who deserves to have bad things happen to you.

CHAPTER FIVE

I CHOSE LIFE

A child often believes that the bad thing(s) must have been their fault, because why else would it have happened to them? A child will not usually blame the predator; they will blame themselves because this is safer than seeing the truth of the person who hurt them, especially if that person is someone they love. Trauma teaches us to glorify the predator when we really need to learn to praise the survivor.

I didn't want it to be true. I didn't want the pain in my right hip to be due to my body holding the pain of abuse that had occurred nearly thirty years earlier. Who would want to believe that their grandfather had sexually abused them at six years of age, and younger? I kept hoping my mind was making it up and that I was just suffering from delusions. Yes, I know that seems odd to wish I was suffering from delusions, but at the time it seemed preferable to the alternative.

For as far back as I could remember I'd had nightmares, but I figured they were from watching too many horror movies and reading scary books. You know, the *Scary Stories to Tell in the Dark* series and other corny teenage thrillers. Though there were a few that had stayed with me over the years I'd never given them much thought.

For many years I had a recurring nightmare of vampires biting my inner right thigh, but again, I attributed this to the vampire movies I loved when I was young. The scarier and the more psychological they were, the better, the more I would feel like it was happening to me. I was unaware that the vampires in my nightmares and the storylines of each movie were metaphors for what happened to me when I was a child. Each movie and dream was about a female victim escaping death at the hands of a male enemy.

In January 2016, I started having dreams that I would come to realize were actually vivid flashbacks. In them, I was standing in a bedroom by a window overlooking a backyard. It looked like what I vaguely recognized as my grandparents' backyard when I was a young child. I always woke up in a state of panic.

During that dream, I would often become frozen, not able to move my body, arms like overcooked spaghetti noodles, trying to scream but nothing coming out. My husband would try to wake me when he felt my body freeze and shake as I tried unsuccessfully to run or punch someone off me. My elderly cat would climb on my chest and paw at my face to wake me up or squeeze my hand with his paw. I swear animals have a sixth sense about these things. They innately understand what we are only starting to comprehend.

One nightmare terrified me so deeply that I woke up drenched in sweat. My entire family was in a house I didn't recognize. We were getting ready to leave. I was upstairs and everyone else was downstairs. I was standing in a room in front of a mirror. I heard my family yell for me to hurry up and come down.

I looked in the mirror and saw my grandfather standing behind me. He had been dead for many years at this point so it startled me. As he started to yell at me in the mirror, my dad immediately appeared in the bedroom. He said to his father, "Leave her alone. This is between you and me." Then he told me, "Kate, go downstairs. I will handle this."

I recall waking up after that dream, calling my dad, and telling him he had some unfinished business to work out with his father. Little did I know what this dream really meant and how it would become the unraveling of my life as I knew it.

Over the next several months, more dreams and flashbacks would come. Each time I was in that room, looking out of a window. Each time I would sense something different. Each time my body would freeze. The panic became so much that I feared going to sleep. I was scared that something more was going to happen in my dreams so I didn't want to sleep. I'd never had sleep issues before.

It's no coincidence that in January I had attended a training aimed at deepening my understanding of the mind, body, spirit connection, and with the intent of gaining some further insight into why "I am the way I am." During that training we did a day of mediumship, where we connected to a crossed-over loved one and received guidance, messages, and wisdom that was available for us. By that point I had been working as a medium for a couple years and the spirit world was as real to me as the human world. As I sat with my partner across from me, I asked God to bring through whomever I needed to hear from and whatever message was needed at this time. I called on the Light of Christ to ensure that only the light of love was allowed.

My partner and I stared at each other, connecting through our eyes, then our teacher had us close our eyes and allow Spirit to bring our loved one through. When I opened my eyes and looked down, her hands had changed into those of an older man, strong like a bear. I looked up and her eyes were now deep brown and her face had taken the shape of Kent, our family's shaman, who left this physical world in August 2009. I remembered that day like it was yesterday. I had gone into a deep meditation on my couch. It was not intentional. I was exhausted. In the meditation, Kent came to me. He said he needed my help to help him cross over. That it was his time. That he could help so many more from the Spirit Realm than he could in his human body. I promised him I would support him as he had supported me in coming back into my human body when I died ten years earlier.

I began to feel all his symptoms – shortness of breath, wheezing, tightness. I fell deep into a transcendent state. I woke up an hour later to a phone call from my mom telling me Kent had passed just a bit ago. I already knew.

Connecting with him now, I immediately felt tears streaming down my cheeks and I felt the heart resonance of a man who had helped my family in so many ways. Our teacher then asked the spirit to give us our message. The message I heard was, "I'm sorry if I ever made you think it was not your choice. You chose to come back."

At those words, my body instantly froze and fountains of tears poured down my cheeks. My body hunched over and I was crippled in heartache.

"What?!" I asked in shock. "I chose to come back? Wait a minute. You told me that you had to make the choice for me. You told me that I was not sure what I wanted to do."

But Kent was gone, and I was once again looking at the face of my partner. I could tell she was confused, but I was not in the space to tell her of the long journey about my death experience. (Yes, I will tell you, but later in this book.)

After the exercise was over, the teacher asked us if we had any questions about our experience. I raised my hand, not even knowing I was doing so.

"So, I had this experience many years ago that I don't really want to go into detail about, but a really big piece of information just came through that there is no way my partner could have known...

When I was eighteen and a freshman in college at Arizona State University, I took what I thought was ecstasy with my boyfriend at the time. It was actually a cocktail drug of seventeen different methamphetamines, and I overdosed, died twice in the hospital, and really shouldn't be alive today."

"Well, that's not true," my teacher replied, "or you wouldn't be here, but I understand what you are saying. So what happened today?"

"My partner gave me a message from my past healer, Kent, who died in 2009. He said that I chose to come back. So, here's the deal. After this all happened in 1999, he told me that when I was in between worlds, I told him I was tired, that I was not sure I wanted to come back. That I wanted to go to sleep. He told me that he had to go against my free will to bring me back because I was not done here yet. I have lived the past seventeen years thinking that I didn't completely choose to be here. That someone else made a very important choice for me. Am I now to believe that I chose to be here? Did I misinterpret what he said to me back then?"

"Sweetie, I can understand why this is so upsetting to you. I also understand, and KNOW, that no one can go against our own free will on our behalf. From what I am receiving, at the time, you were still not fully back in your human body, and your ego-mind interpreted his message as saying he chose for you. What I am hearing from him is that he assisted you in coming back because you were afraid of being human again."

"This changes so much..." I said, then fell silent.

"It could, or it may not," she said, smiling at me with her knowing gaze of compassion. Looking back, I realize she knew it *was* going to change a lot. So did I; I just didn't know what that meant or how it was going to affect me.

As I reflected on this information over the next day that yes, I began to feel this deep need to go through in my mind the past seventeen years and notice how many times I'd wondered how I was able to be alive.

Why me? Why did I survive that tragedy while so many others don't make it? Why was I given another chance when I didn't want it? Did I want it? I recall at that time not really knowing. So many questions spiraled through my mind.

The training ended on a Saturday. As I often would after such an intense training, I knew I needed some time to integrate, to reflect, to just be. The next day, Sunday, nothing unusual was happening. I planned the day off so I could rest, recharge and be with my family.

CHAPTER SIX

TRIGGERED

I was heading into my bathroom, and as I came out, I heard my husband, Eric, say, "Kate, I think we lost Bella."

"What do you mean? Who let her out?" I panicked. I don't let my cats outside.

"No, Kate. I think we *lost* her."

I came around the corner into the master bedroom to see my calico of fifteen years lying dead on the floor. I screamed in terror, horror, as I fell down beside her. Lupo, my long-haired Russian blue cat and Bella's lifelong love, was next to her too, as was Eric.

Shaking and trembling, I picked up her body and rocked her back and forth, hugging her close to my heart, sobbing into her fur.

"No!" I yelled, "Not my Bella!"

My two young kids came rushing into the room.

"Mom, are you okay? We heard you scream. What's wrong with Bella?"

I couldn't talk. I was transported back in time to when I was sixteen and my parents were away at one of our vacation homes in Montana. My younger sister and I were staying home with my older cousin, who was babysitting us. The morning they left my mom had told me that Spud, our Maine Coon cat, had not come home yet – not a huge deal as he often went out all day and some-times stayed out overnight. He always returned the next morning to eat.

I was arriving home from being out with friends. There was a message on our answering machine. It was from our neighbors. "Hi, Lombardo family. I think your cat is on the side yard between our homes. I'm so sorry."

I ran outside. It was April. The air was freezing and the ground was still somewhat frozen from the Chicago winter. I ran to the side yard between the two houses, which was right outside my bedroom window on the far back right corner of our home.

There he was. Lifeless on the dirt. He looked like he had been bitten by an animal.

I don't remember exactly what happened next. I recall being back inside, calling my brother, Ryan, up at college in Wisconsin. Spud was his cat. He had picked him out at a shelter in Michigan one summer many years earlier.

"Ryan, I found Spud. The neighbors called. He is dead."

"What do you mean he is dead?"

"I found his body. It looks like he was killed by an animal. His body is on the sideyard. I don't know what to do."

"You need to cover his body up. You need to move him."

"I'm not moving him. What should I do? Mom and Dad are out of town and Jenny is not home yet. Mickey is inside with me."

"Go cover him up. Get a box and cover him up. In the morning, you will have to take his body to the vet." I could hear the trembling in his voice.

"It is dark out, Ryan. I don't want to go out there again."

"Kate, I don't care. You have to. No one else is there."

I hung up with him. I took a box from our garage and an old sheet from the linen closet. I put on a jacket and boots. I could barely see. Our yard was lined with trees and there was no light on that side of the house. I took a small flashlight with me (this was long before the time of cell phones with flashlights).

I found his body again and placed the sheet over him. I draped the box on top of him, knowing I would have to get up so early to get him to the vet and then get to school.

Shit, I have to call Mom, I thought, though I don't remember talking to her that night.

The next thing I recall is my bedroom door being pushed open. I jumped up from bed to see my brother.

"Kate, where is he? I went outside and the box was empty. Where did you put Spud's body?"

"Ryan? You're home?"

He had driven down from Wisconsin, a nearly three-hour trip, in the middle of the night, worried about his cat's body.

I threw on a warm jacket and shoes. I went outside with him to find Spud. We looked around the area of the box. We didn't see him. Then I turned to my left and there he was. This time his body was torn in two pieces. I could see his insides now.

"Ryan. He is over here."

"Oh my God. Spud!"

Ryan ran to get a shovel. Neither of us wanted to touch his body. I laid out the sheet, then he scooped Spud up and put him on the sheet. He wrapped him up and placed him in the box. He carried the box to the garage.

"Kate. Tomorrow morning, you need to take his body to the vet. I have to drive back up for school. I need you to do this. Can you do this?"

"Yes. I can do this. I'm so sorry, Ryan. He was the best cat."

He gave me a hug. I went back inside. The next morning I put the box in my car. I drove to the vet, dropped off his body, and drove to another day of my junior year of high school.

"Mom. Mom. MOM?"

"NO! Not Bella. Not Bella. Not Bella." I was back in my bedroom, holding Bella in my arms. Her lifeless body just like Spud's.

I think I held her for an hour. Shaking. Rocking. My kids' scared of my cries and tears of pain. My husband tried to console me, telling me how he'd found her on the floor.

I questioned whether I had walked past her when I went into the bathroom. I questioned if I missed her. I questioned why I didn't know she was sick. I remembered earlier that day she had been breathing funny when she tried to jump up on my daughter's bed. I wondered what I did wrong. Why didn't I know? Did she know I loved her?

After an hour of holding her, Eric told me that it was time to place her body in a box. That he would take her to be cremated the next morning. I told Lupo, my other cat, that it was time to say goodbye.

He walked right over to her and I witnessed the most loving exchange between two animals that I have ever seen. Lupo gave Bella a few kisses on her head, as if bidding her farewell. Then he turned around, walked away, and went under my bed. My sobbing continued as my kids left my bedroom and Eric took Bella to be put in a sheet, inside a box, in the garage. I don't remember much after that.

I woke up that night from an awful nightmare. I was frozen. I couldn't move. I was on my back. My legs felt like lead. I opened my eyes. I saw a dark shadowy figure on the side of my bed in my room. My entire body became cold and solid. I heard the words to a song that every time I hear it, I still get chills down my spine: "Needle in the head, you're going to wind up dead." It was an eerie man's voice. I shivered.

I called on all my spirit guides, God, Jesus, Divine Mother, loved ones, the Light, asking for it to leave, to make it stop. I turned on my nightstand light. No one was there. Eric was sound asleep next to me. Lupo was at my feet. Bella was not. Oh yeah, she was dead.

I kept my light on and snuggled in as tight as I could into Eric's warm body. His energy always grounds me. I don't think I fell back asleep that night.

The nightmares continued. Less and less sleep. More anxiety. More panic.

This loss, and the memory of a loss I'd never dealt with, sent me into the beginning of what would be a spiraling down to find myself once again. The weeks that followed included events so challenging that I swear God must have thought I was super woman, and they just kept on coming.

In early February, I was diagnosed with systemic candida and had to go under an intense treatment protocol to clear my system of this fungal overgrowth. At the same time our twelve-year-old lab, Jager, suddenly became ill and we were days from losing him too.

It was all too much for my being, and I started having multiple panic attacks a day, could not eat, was sinking into a deep depression and not even knowing it.

I prayed that God would spare us this loss as we had not recovered from the sudden death of Bella. Miraculously, Jager recovered for a short time.

I lost twenty-five pounds in six weeks and was not interested in anything. I made myself go to work, see my clients, all the while living in a haze of an existence. I was barely able to get out of bed, my body started shaking all the time. My doctor wanted me to take Xanax, but I was too afraid from all the horror stories I'd heard from clients and friends trying to come off of those medications. Instead, I started using different herbal remedies but nothing helped.

I slowly distanced myself from my family, not calling my parents as I normally would, not texting friends or even returning their texts. At night, I would eat dinner with my kids and husband, then go into my room, take a bath, journal, and sleep. I had no energy and no interest in anything else. I was fading away.

Early in March, I woke up startled. Something was different. My body started shaking and my throat felt like it was closing, I knew something was wrong. It was not the racing-thought, teeth-clenching kind of anxiety I was familiar with.

My mind raced with thoughts: "Am I safe? Is he going to hurt me again? Who is he? Why can't I move my legs? What the fuck is happening to my body?!" Terror was replaying through the sensations of my being, even though my eyes were open and I could see that I was laying in my bedroom alone, totally safe, with Lupo by my side.

I was entering some strange yet viscerally known territory. My body was reliving something foreign to my adult mind but very familiar to the young child still living in me.

Some of my family came from Chicago to visit me and quickly realized that something was very wrong. My dad, with whom I had developed a very close spiritual relationship in my young adult years, said to me, "Katie (he is one of two people in my life who call me that), it is as if someone turned off your light. It is gone. Your eyes are dark. Your light is off. What is going on?"

My older sister, Suzy, pulled me into my bedroom, and for an hour proceeded to try and bring me back to life. Our relationship had its trials over the years, but she was often the one who could speak life back into me, who could bring me to see things from a new perspective, who could care for me and understand me in a way that not many could, but not that day. It was then that she knew I needed more help, and I knew it too.

My parents called on the help of a friend they'd met years earlier at spiritual meetings at Kent's home. This friend was a licensed therapist and also a shaman in her own right. I called her the next day to schedule an appointment. I would see her a few days later.

My heart knew I needed help. My brain would flip from rational, conscious understanding to emotional turmoil and confusion, where I did not understand why the tools I had gathered over many years of yoga and meditation training were not enough to bring me into a state of clarity and groundedness.

It was as if every tool in my toolbox was dull, broken, or unable to fit into the hole that I was drowning in at every moment. Insights of clarity would come, followed by complete fog and dissolution. At times I felt so calm and integrated, and at others it was all I could do to remember to breathe.

My body became a foreign territory with no map included on how to navigate the numerous, strange sensations I was experiencing. My mind became my enemy as I tried to understand what I was feeling and make sense of it all. At times when I needed positive, healthy self-talk, my mind would instead create horror stories of possibilities, most of which included me dying of cancer or some rare disease. As much as I tried to control my thoughts, there was something inside me brewing a horrific storm and for a while I thought I was strong enough to handle it on my own. I was wrong.

My first therapy session was informative and grounding. I found myself pouring my heart out to this woman whom I'd just met and yet had somehow known for a long time. We agreed that I would meet with her once a week to begin to put the pieces of my heart back together. She described it like going into a dark closet to begin to organize all the clutter. I explained that I had already done a lot of shadow work in the yoga therapy training I did five years prior. As I shared with her about that training and inner work, she had this look on her face of understanding and a sideways smile as if her eyes knew something I did not.

I clearly remember her saying, "Ahhh… I understand now. There was a big piece that either they forgot to teach you or that you were unable to receive in the teachings at that time. What is the first thing you do when you are going into the dark closet to search for something?"

"I don't know. You open the door."

"Yes, that, but then what?"

I stared with a blank face, completely annoyed and frustrated with this ridiculous metaphor.

"You turn on the light," she replied with a soft gaze and smile.

Of course! Of course you turn on the light or how else can you see? I thought, my rational mind once again conflicting with the emotional shitstorm that would overtake my brain. The problem was, it felt as if the switch was broken and I could not find any backup batteries for the flashlight that I had used for so many years. I was searching in the dark – for what, I did not know – and allowing the past to become the crumbling bedrock upon which I had to choose to live or slowly die.

I have a pretty amazing relationship with God, now. At that time, I was deeply connected to my spirituality and would call on my guides, angels, God, et cetera, but I did not yet have the connection to my source of life through my body - so often when I called on these forces it felt esoteric and mystical, not embodied and living.

I often wondered where God was during all this time of suffering and pain. Why was I going through all this? Why did He allow these horrible things to happen? What greater purpose must there be to this awful time?

Let's be honest, nothing during that time seemed fruitful, purposeful, or intentional. It felt like someone had taken a scalpel to my insides and had a death grip on the little bit of beauty that I was clinging to each day that I woke up.

Dramatic? Yes. True? Yes.

Just as I was starting to feel a little bit more alive after a couple of weeks of therapy, our chocolate lab, Jager, started feeling very sick once again. Over a two-week period, his health would slowly fade and I felt myself slipping deeper into despair with each of his last breaths.

By Easter weekend Jager was nearing his end, and giving us many signs that it was his time to go. As a family we chose to spend

Easter Sunday loving him and being by his side every moment that we could. I took him outside to our front patio and sat with him on the path up to our front door. He laid at my right side, feeling the sun, and looking out at the street that we'd lived on for seven years. My hand rested on his belly, gently petting him as tears poured down my cheeks, knowing this would be the last time we would spend a day in the sun together, simply enjoying the wind and sun on our skin. I told him how much I would miss him, and all the memories over the years where his smell and love permeated into my heart.

My best friend was dying right before my eyes and my heart was collapsing inside my chest. I tried to be strong for him. I did not want him to remember me this way and see me in tears during the last hours we had together in this life.

As I cried, he would look up at me, panting hard, breath labored, as if reminding me to be present and feel, not focus on the next day or the past but to breathe into that moment and remember the love he gave. We talked that day for a long time about all the memories we shared – walking at the park, when he chewed up five of my left shoes (yes, just the left of five pairs), when we brought Connor home from the hospital and the two instantly formed an unbreakable bond, even to the point of "Ager" being Connor's first word. The memories flipped through my mind like a scrapbook in time.

That night I prayed. I prayed God would give me a sign that was very clear that we were making the right choice in laying him to rest the next day. Over a period of a few hours, Jager's condition continued to worsen. It culminated in a bedroom full of bloody stool all over our floor and him whining in pain. My heart knew what my mind was having a hard time processing. We had to put him down the next morning.

I spent all night holding him and cuddling him on my bedroom floor, exactly where Bella died just a couple of months before.

The next morning Eric called our vet and told him of our decision; by ten a.m. we were at the office. Our vet was a kind, gentle man who deeply loved Jager, and although he knew we were making the right decision for him, he cried at the loss he knew we were facing, and for his own heart.

Jager knew what was happening. He sat down and allowed the vet to give him the shot to calm his nerves. Within minutes he was laying on his right side, with me holding him on the ground and Eric at his head, both of us in tears as we both spoke our final farewells. I laid next to him with my left hand on his side and began to sing Snatam Kaur's "Long time sun" into his sweet ears. His breathing shallowed and his body got soft. He started deeply relaxing. The vet came back into the room and told us it was time.

How this man does this for a living I have no idea. An angel in human form with the job of trying to save our beloved animal friends, yet also having to be the one to help bring them into deeper peace, is a job my heart cannot fathom. I am grateful for these beings who choose to serve in this way.

He placed the tourniquet on Jager's left paw and told us it would only take a minute or so for him to cross over. I continued to sing to him and Eric and I cried, saying goodbye to the best friend who was by our side through all the love and heartache of twelve years together.

The vet injected the medicine to help him pass, and within thirty seconds, I felt this huge rush of energy by the left side of my body. He was gone. The vet confirmed it at that moment. My sweet baby boy was gone and I felt desolate, scared, and so unsure how I would make it through this grief after such a hard couple of months.

Eric and I took the day off work, and we drove out to the lake and sat in tears, numb with grief and sorrow and trying to find meaning in all the pain.

The next few days were a blur of emotion. I struggled to be present in my body, same as most days, but the symptoms were different and getting bigger. My body was constantly shaking; I was always cold and tired; and my mind was a fog, yet my business continued to grow. People were seeking me to help them with their suffering while I was in the midst of my own tornado. I felt like a fraud.

I had this pit-in-my-stomach feeling that God was trying to give me a message I could not understand. I prayed. I meditated. I journaled. I did my yoga practice. I walked. I took more baths than in probably all my adult life. I heard these words, "I have shaken you to awaken you."

Well, great. What was I waking up to? Why wasn't I better yet? What did better even mean?

CHAPTER SEVEN

UPROOTED

I managed to get through the month of April, seeing my therapist and trying to navigate this season of life. The nightmares continued and many nights were sleepless and scary. I chose to walk away from co-ownership of my yoga studio that I'd been part of since 2011. I didn't have the strength to manage all the piling responsibilities in my life, and something had to go. I just couldn't do it all anymore.

During my therapy sessions, there was more unraveling of the stories of my past. We started talking about my fears of sexual intimacy and she couldn't understand why this was an issue. As she said, nothing I had shared with her had any correlation to intimacy issues. It was true; though I had shared with her the traumas of my teenage years, beginning with finding out I was moving to Arizona the summer before my senior year of high school and, I had not mentioned what happened in the spring of 1998.

It began one day in February, when my parents were in Arizona visiting Kent and his family, who had moved there the year prior. I'd joked with them about buying a house and moving there, saying I would be okay with it, but never really thinking they would ever do such a thing. It was a flippant statement made at a time when I was frustrated with my friends and teenage existence.

I'd lived in the same town my whole life. It was the only home I knew, where I thought lifelong friendships were being made, and where I thought my family would stay forever. It was the kind of town where many knew your name, where you knew the timing of stoplights, where there was one high school, with many neighboring schools just a town away. The kind of town where the police had nothing better to do on a Friday night than bust high school parties and try and catch you for breaking curfew. As much as I complained about it, I loved it. My heart felt comfortable there, and it was all I knew.

One evening I was at home with my younger sister and my cousin, who was babysitting us while my parents were away. I remember them calling, though I can't recall the exact conversation. I think I conveniently repressed it aside from a few choice words.

"Kate. We bought a house. We are moving in June to Scottsdale."

I am not sure what I said, but since I was a great people-pleaser at the time I'm sure it was something kind. I hung up the phone, grabbed the keys to my car, and headed as fast as I could to one of my best friends to cry and tell her the awful news. My parents were dragging me sixteen hundred miles away from the only home and the only people I'd ever known – including my three older siblings and friends I'd had since kindergarten. They were taking away my senior year.

My only experience of Arizona was a short vacation to Scottsdale with my mom, dad, and younger sister. We stayed in some fancy resort and I did recall loving the sight of palm trees and mountains. I also loved visiting the magical town of Sedona, about two hours away.

Aside from Kent and his family being there, I could only imagine the reasons my parents wanted to relocate to Arizona. Dad had recently retired from a big corporate position and was going through a midlife crisis while trying to support his family and get over the depression of not making the money he once did.

My perception was that he was trying to find who he was on the inside, rather than this life he had created on the outside.

I resented my parents for this move, for the loss of my senior year with my childhood friends, the loss of memories and important rites of passage, and of time with my siblings who lived in the Midwest. I would have years of nightmares of wandering the halls of the high school, visiting my locker from junior year, trying to say goodbye to that time in my life and reclaim the missing pieces lost to a selfish decision.

When I was eleven or twelve years old, my dad was diagnosed with high cholesterol. I am sharing this with you secondhand as I overheard most of it, not told directly. The doctors put him on a medicine to lower his cholesterol, and one of the side effects was damaging his liver. His health was deteriorating and doctors didn't know what to do aside from increasing the cholesterol meds to try and control that at the cost of Dad's liver.

At the time, my brother Ryan, was playing football in high school and had hurt his knee. His girlfriend asked him if he would be open to seeing her uncle, "a healer," and Ryan said yes. This is how Kent came into our lives.

Kent was able to fix my brother's knee, and told him he could help our father as well. Mind you, Kent didn't know Dad or anything about his condition. Ryan told Dad what Kent said and, after convincing him that he had not revealed any information, Dad agreed to go.

Dad writes of his visit in great detail in his book, *Vision of Eagle, Strength of Bear*. For our purposes here I'll share that Mom went with him to that first appointment, and Kent embraced them both as if they were long-lost friends. They met his wife, Randy, a radiologist, and two young kids. Kent was an artist and teacher by education, and despite great resistance had accepted his calling as a shamanic healer. As he said, he hadn't gone looking for a teacher, as many seekers do; his teacher came to him.

Kent prescribed certain herbs and holistic remedies for Dad to help get his health back on track. After carefully researching each one he finally decided to give them a try, while still taking the meds from his western doctors. When his next round of blood-work finally showed positive improvements, the doctors wanted to increase his meds again. He told them he was done taking their meds and was going to use the herbs and supplements instead, as they were what was causing the difference.

Kent, Randy, and my parents began a journey of close friend-ship. Dad's health greatly improved, and through Kent my parents were connected with a community of adults unlike any I had ever seen. They were social, happier, more lively at home, and tak-ing time to reconnect to their Spirit. Growing up Catholic, there was always a connection to God or at least the expectation of the belief. This was different.

Kent opened something up in my parents that had been dor-mant for many decades. They would go each Saturday night to a metaphysical group for meditations, food, and socializing, and Kent would often channel one of several light beings. I remember going a few times and being in awe and wonder at the conversa-tions, the laughter, the smiles on my parents' faces. It brought me a lot of joy to see them so happy and with friends. This was a side to them I wasn't used to seeing. Our lives shifted from religious to spiritual, and I saw my parents make some major changes in life that seemed drastic yet, from what I could tell, made them happy.

Over the years the relationship grew into more family-oriented than friendship. I babysat their kids, and our families enjoyed each other's company. I share later in this book how Kent helped me heal from an ACL surgery, how he helped when I overdosed and died, and how he supported me during postpartum and mental/emotional struggles after having my son. Kent would eventually become my first teacher on the Archangels, homeopathy, chakras, meditation, herbal supplements, the energy bodies, meridians, channeling, how withheld emotions cause physical disease, how to access Christ-consciousness, how to move energy, how to calm my nervous system in times of stress, and more on energy medicine. His gifts and teachings helped guide me while he was here on Earth, and they continued to do so after he was in Spirit.

When Kent and Randy moved to Arizona, I saw my parents start to decline. They were less social, more distant, and more unhappy. I knew they missed their friends and metaphysical community. It was not a common group in the North Shore of Chicago at that time.

Because of this I justified my parents' decision to move to Scottsdale, even though it meant uprooting me at a critical time in my life and drastically changing their own. I wanted nothing to do with it, and made that known. Friends offered for me to live with them during my senior year, but my parents said no. There was no negotiating with them on this. I tried.

I finished out my junior year pretty angry, getting drunk a lot at high school parties, keeping great grades so my parents wouldn't worry, and pretending I was okay, though inside I was destroyed and in complete fear of what was to come. While the move to Arizona would eventually bring much beauty and love into my life, at age seventeen it was the beginning of a season of trauma.

CHAPTER EIGHT

RAPE

My therapist empathized, never understanding why my parents did that to me either. It was very healthy for me to have another adult hold this compassionate space about a time in my life that many others wrote off as not that big of a deal. Kids often have to move with their parents, they said. She helped me clarify that the unmet emotional needs of that experience locked it into my nervous system as a trauma. Her process was to work on a new perception of the experience, which I already had. I knew I was blessed to have met my husband and great friends, yet I still couldn't find my way out of the pain. She inquired again about sexual intimacy, not understanding why I struggled with feeling safe to be intimate in my marriage.

I then shared with her something I had not shared with many at that time. In April of 1998, after attending the prom together, I had been raped by my then-boyfriend. We had previously had sex one time. He was my first.

Prom was fine – nothing noteworthy about the actual event. There was a dinner at a restaurant way too expensive for teenage kids, followed by a dance at a fancy hotel in downtown Chicago. The plan was for everyone in our party to spend the night at our friend's home (I'll call her Gwen), then travel the next day up to a lake where another friend – I'll call her Judy – had a house.

We got back to Gwen's place after the dance, and all of us, about twenty people, went into the basement. Basements in the Midwest are a big thing, and often where high school kids get into the most trouble. There was drinking, pot, and I'm sure some other drugs that I was unaware of at the time.

The basement was large, with a big living area, a bar, and another room built off the living space. I was drinking, again, but not unaware of what was going on around me. The night came to an end and we got all set up to sleep. My boyfriend had found us a spot to sleep near the back of the bar.

As I went to lay down, with a little too much to drink in my system, my head and upper body were close to being under a chair. I recall him coming to lay by me and saying he wanted to have sex.

I said, "No. There are too many people around. I don't want to."

He persisted.

Again, I said no.

He climbed on top of me, pushing my head and chest now under the above-mentioned chair so I was caged in from my head to my ribs. He pulled off my pants, and I dissociated. I remember seeing it from above. I wish I had kicked him off me. I wish I had punched, kicked, screamed, yelled. I wished someone would have pulled him off me. Didn't they hear me say no? Didn't *he* hear me say no? He raped me with eighteen other people within a few feet of us.

He finished and I passed out.

I woke up angry. Pissed. I barely talked to him. He knew I was mad, and I am guessing he was unaware why.

We drove out to the lake house pretty much in silence. I wanted to go home but I could not find the words. What I would come to realize was a common theme in my life. Years of trauma had already stolen my voice and power to choose what was best for me.

When we arrived I avoided him as much as I could. The tents were set up. More drinking, partying, going on boats on the lake, playing games, ensued. That night he tried to have sex with me in the tent. This time I was not drunk. Somehow, I knew better. He was pissed at me that I wouldn't have sex with him so he left the tent. I went to sleep. He drove me home the next day. I broke up with him the next week, saying that I was moving and he was going to college so there was no point in continuing our relationship.

I never confronted him about that night. I didn't even call it rape until two friends said to me when I was sharing this story well into my early thirties: "Kate. You were raped that night."

"Yes. Kate. You were raped that night," my therapist confirmed. I was sitting on her black leather couch in her home office replaying the story to her. She asked why I didn't fight. Why didn't I push him off? I know. Not the best things for a therapist to ask. I did not know why, but that epiphany would come later.

As she tried to help me process this experience, she worked at the level of the mind, however, with my training as a yoga therapist, I knew that this was deeper than that. All the things she was sharing with me were true, and my mind knew they were true. I had the tools. So why could I not connect the dots, make the necessary perceptions changes, shift my awareness, heal and move forward?

I proceeded to keep seeing her, making some progress each week only to feel like I had taken eight steps back. Little climb, huge fall. Something was not connecting. Something was not shifting. I was in moments of clarity and large spans of storms.

My doctor put me on progesterone, thinking my hormones were low due to a blood test. She thought that might help the anxiety levels. She also had me start taking some new herbal formulas to help support my nervous system. She still wanted me to take the Xanax. I still said no.

In 2017, I would end up processing this rape experience with my first trauma therapist in an EMDR session. My therapist asked me to lay on her couch, buzzing EMDR tappers in hand, and she guided me to scan my body to see where I was holding the memory of this rape. Instantly my upper back had intense pain, then localized in my right shoulder. This pain became the doorway to enter the memory and change the story.

I began to breathe as she guided me through a simple relaxation technique to calm my nervous system. I invited Jesus and Mother Mary to join me on this journey inward to reclaim a part of me left behind during this rape. As soon as the buzzing tappers turned on, I was standing in that basement as my adult self. No one was there except seventeen-year-old me, stuck under the chair, frozen in the same position for nineteen years. Jesus and Mary were with me. I slowly walked over to my frozen body. Jesus asked me if I needed help. I said, "No, I need to do this."

I took the chair off my body, and in the EMDR session my body jolted. I was okay, and my therapist checked to make sure. I was communicating with her what was happening in this multi-dimensional space the entire time. I went and scooped up the seventeen-year-old me, letting her know that she was safe now. He couldn't hurt her anymore. Everyone was gone, and we had come to rescue her. My eyes opened and I saw the pain and hurt. I saw the fear and shock.

Jesus helped me get her up to standing. She knew who He was and felt a little angry at Him for not being there that night. She also knew who I was and was curious about how so many years had gone by. That conversation would come later once she was safe.

I walked myself towards the basement stairs, Mary in front of me and Jesus at my side. I told them, "I am not going up those stairs with her. Find us another way out of here."

Instantly the wall to my left opened up like a portal and Mary led us through into my sacred garden and safe space. I walked my seventeen-year-old self over to a soft lounge to lay down. I sat with her on her left side, and Jesus on her right. Tears were pouring down my cheeks as I grieved the pain and hurt I felt in that moment.

I quickly reflected back on the basement and it was empty, just a cold, gray room with a bar and old concrete floors. I was no longer stuck there.

I returned awareness to myself and seventeen-year-old me.

Jesus said to me, "Kate, I will take care of her for now. She needs time to rest and restore. I will help her."

Mary said, "She's been through so much and I will help, too."

Jesus continued, "When it's time, she will integrate into wholeness with you. For now, you did good, my child. Let yourself rest."

I took some deep breaths and opened my eyes. My therapist was crying as she witnessed this sacred act of self-love. I rescued a part of myself that day. I would do so many, many times over the next several years.

CHAPTER NINE

THE BODY SPEAKS

On May 3, 2016, I headed for a private session with my mentor. I had scheduled it weeks prior, hoping that she would be able to help me, since when I did the training with her in January, it opened up some of this shift. I was not holding her responsible, just hoping she could help.

I arrived at her healing center looking forward to our four hours together. I wanted to talk with her about my business, about my mental/emotional states, about my books. She invited me in to sit down on her couch in the main space of the center. It was a very informal space with so much love.

As we sat down, she smiled her beautiful, big smile and said, "So, whatcha want to talk about?"

Out of nowhere I started talking about my right hip pain. I told her that I'd had this pain since I was pregnant with Connor ten years earlier. I shared that I had been struggling mentally, physically, emotionally since the training. I shared about my nightmares and flashbacks. I told her that I was starting to wonder if I had been sexually abused as a child.

She looked at me with a lot of love and said, "Well, you're an embodiment practitioner. You work with the body. Have you asked your body?"

I laughed a little. "No. I have not asked my body."

"Why don't you close your eyes, bring attention to the right hip pain, and ask your body what it wants you to know."

I closed my eyes and guided my attention into the sensation of my right hip. That constant ache of a rubber band being stretched too thin yet never breaking.

In an instant I was back in time. I was six years old. I was laying on a bed that I did not recognize. My right hip was being pushed down by *him*. Who was it? My grandfather. My paternal grand-father. I hated that man and at that moment I knew why. I was a child. I don't know all of what he did to me. I have memories of being touched inappropriately. I watched it all happen. There was a floral bedspread, a window to my left, a dresser on the wall in front of the bed. He kept pushing my right hip down. It hurt. I couldn't move. He threatened me. I was terrified of him. He was a monster. My body started shaking intensely as I sat on her couch.

Knowing I had to move this energy out of my body, I quickly brought myself onto the floor of her living room. I placed my body in a yoga pose, called prone pigeon with my right leg back and left leg forward. I needed to open up my right hip flexor.

I went back into the memory. My mentor came beside me on the floor and sent Reiki and love into my being. Over the course of the next forty minutes, my body had complete memory recall of the sexual abuse. I finally understood that scene from my nightmares. I was standing in the bedroom, in shock, looking out the bedroom window, staring at what I finally understood was my grandparent's backyard. I heard him say, "Get out now. We are done."

I walked out of the bedroom, turned left, went down the short hall and proceeded down the stairs. Where were my parents, I wondered?

I was still on the living room floor, in the yoga pose, shaking violently as my hip released the trapped trauma that had been liv-ing inside of me for over thirty years. What did all this mean?

Tears poured down my cheeks. So many questions swirling through my mind. At that moment there was so much confusion, yet a sense of relief flooded through my being as I felt as though I finally uncovered the missing piece of my past. A sense of anger, no rage, began to curse through my blood, wondering if he had hurt my sisters too. I was filled with fury and wanted revenge. I wanted him to hurt. I prayed he was in hell suffering for the horrific pain he caused me and probably many others. What about my cousins? There were so many girls. Did he do this to the boys, my brothers, too? Who else?

Why did my parents allow us to spend time with him? Did they know he did this to me? Where were they? Why did they let this happen to me? Why didn't they protect me and my siblings from this man?

I had so many questions, and did the best I could to stay present to the pain. The physical pain was dissolving. The emotional pain was birthing.

When I left her house that day, I don't remember what I did. I know I told Eric. I don't remember anything else. I was completely dissociated, even doing my best to stay in my body.

At my next therapy appointment I told my therapist all of this. She was incredibly sad for me, and grateful. I remember her saying, "Kate, this is the missing piece. It finally all makes sense."

Well, I was so glad it made sense to her because nothing made sense to me.

"Kate, I didn't know you when you overdosed, but I remember being told the story. After hearing about the rape at seventeen, and knowing what I do know about the overdose, it all makes sense now. Most of the time a girl who has chosen to be with men who harm her has some kind of background in childhood abuse or trauma. I know your parents and I know that was not the case with them. Now I understand. Now you can heal. This is the root cause of the rest of the symptoms. Your body finally revealed to you the cause of this pain. This is amazing!"

I, too, was very grateful for my body's ability to finally unlock the root cause of this pain. I was also very aware that while my hip no longer hurt, my heart and mind were aching in a new way, and the intrusive thoughts only continued to become worse. I would come to remember sexual abuse at the hands of my paternal grandfather all the way back to two years of age. This memory at six years old was the last time.

My nervous system was unwinding faster than I could handle the process. I was living very out of body, and not able to handle daily life. I continued in weekly therapy, stressing over the large amount of money being spent each week for my recovery, yet I wasn't getting better.

My doctor begged me to take the Xanax. I caved. It helped for about three hours at a time. She questioned why I was so adamant about not taking meds. I had a tendency to not share all of my medical background with my doctors. I just didn't think they would believe me or understand. I knew that was about to change, and it was time to let my doctor, who I needed to trust, in on this story.

I shared with her what happened on December 11, 1999. Only my family and some close friends knew this about me.

CHAPTER TEN

RESURRECTED LIFE

I was eighteen and a freshman in college at Arizona State University. It was finals weekend (Saturday, December 11, to be exact), and I and the guy I was dating were going to a party at the house of one of his friends.

My boyfriend, who I had met my senior year of high school while still reeling from the move to Scottsdale, was a not-so-nice guy. He was transient, from a broken home and childhood, and always meeting strange people. He was also not the kind of person my parents and my friends liked, however, I believed I was in love with him, and him me. Love was unsafe then, which is why I can now name that it was not love. Remembering the childhood sexual abuse helped me to understand why I would have fallen for a guy like him. I was never safe with him, yet he reminded my nervous system of the same energy I'd come to believe was love.

He and I decided we were going to do ecstasy together that night. We had used it once before and it was a great experience. While visiting my parents' house that day I asked Dad for money, and he gave it to me without question, probably thinking I just needed some extra pocket cash. I was using it to pay for the drugs. He also thought I was going back to the dorm to study, not out partying with my boyfriend at the home of some guy I had only met once.

It took a long time to forgive myself for that lie.

I left my parents after dinner and headed to pick up my boyfriend. We went straight to this house in the far Northwest side of Phoenix, an hour away from my dorm room in Tempe where my friends were studying for finals. A part of me knew that is where I should have been.

I walked into the house and saw several guys I didn't know. I was the only girl. Had I had known better, I would have listened to that tightening in my belly and numbness in my legs. I didn't know better. I was an expert at dissociating from it.

The entry to the home was wide and opened up to a living room/kitchen combo. When you walked in, the kitchen was on the left and the living room right in front of you. There was a small step down, I think, after the entryway.

I recognized two of the guys, who I had met before through my boyfriend. Both seemed nice. One of my friends was supposed to meet up with us but she wasn't answering her phone. My very best friend was at our dorm studying and tried to get me to stay in that night. She hated my boyfriend. From the time I met him I started making some bad choices, and no matter what family or friends told me, I wanted to be with him. I remembered Dad trying to tell me that it was a high school relationship and would end before college. That only added fuel to my fire.

I grabbed a beer while waiting for the ecstasy to arrive. It seemed there was some problem getting it so it would be delayed. Again, another sign that I wasn't making the best choice. Again, I ignored it.

My boyfriend asked me to come into the garage. They turned on some dance music. A few of us started dancing. Loud music. Flickering lights.

A couple of the guys were going to grab more beer. I wanted to go with them. One of the guys I knew drove. My boyfriend took the front passenger seat. That was strange, I thought. Why wasn't he sitting with me? Some other guy sat in the back seat next to me. I was behind the driver.

We went to a local gas station for beer. Then I recall the driver saying, "Want to see something cool?"

He drove us up to some mountain lookout area. He had me get out of the car.

I was standing at the edge of the mountain looking at thousands of stars.

Every time I look at the stars I stare between them, at the space between. The blackness. The void. The beyond the beyond. Ever since I was a kid I wondered what was beyond the beyond. In the darkness. In the black. What was holding all the stars in place. I used to want to be an astronaut. "Space Camp" was my favorite movie for a long time; escaping Earth sounded exciting and safer than being on it. We got back in the car, and when we arrived at the house, dancing continued.

They called us, my boyfriend and me, into the house. The drugs had arrived, delivered by a woman I had met once before. There were three of us taking ecstasy, and I recall seeing the three pills in the woman's hand. She was standing at the entryway of the home right inside the front door. She held out her hand to my boyfriend, me, and the one other guy. I remember clearly thinking that these pills looked totally different than the ecstasy I had taken about a month prior. I took it anyway. We each took one. She and her friend left. I went back to dancing in the garage, knowing it took a bit to sink in.

After more dancing, I came inside and stood over the kitchen sink. I was warm and starting to really feel the effects of the drug. I remember people sitting on the couches. My boyfriend was standing opposite the large kitchen island from me.

I said, "This stuff is amazing!"

The rest of what happened to me is a combination of hearsay from my boyfriend, my parents, and Kent; my direct remembrance from in-between worlds; and, over time, through visceral memory, flashbacks, somatic memories, dreams, nightmares, and trauma therapy.

The following is what my boyfriend shared with me. I have no memory of any of it.

> At that moment I fell into seizures on the kitchen floor. It was a little after one a.m. They didn't call the paramedics. Instead they placed me in the master bedroom alone.
>
> When he came back in the room I was unconscious on the bed and having seizures. He was trying to keep me from choking on my tongue while seizing. He said he even stuck his hand in my mouth to pull up my tongue. I was in full epileptic seizures continuously. (I had never had a seizure prior in my life.)
>
> At one point he said I threw up everywhere. He proceeded to undress me down to my bra and underwear. After a few hours, he said I lost complete control of my urine and bowels. At this point he said he put me in the tub. Mind you, I was still seizing.
>
> He said he wanted to call 911 but the people he was with forbade it. You will understand why they felt this way later. Finally after I had been seizing and unconscious for over thirteen hours, they called 911.
>
> This was all I learned from him. Here is what I remember when I woke up:

I looked to my left and saw Jesus sitting in a large chair next to my hospital bed, although at that time I did not know I was in the hospital. I woke up again and saw Kent sitting in that same chair. He was smiling, twirling his pendulum. He said, "It's good to see you again." I fell back asleep. My next memory is the face of a nurse pushing my hospital bed down a cold hallway, the bright fluorescent lights blinding me. I was going for testing.

I finally woke up fully in a hospital room. I looked around and saw friends and family. I told them I needed to go take my finals, then, feeling my neck, asked where my jewelry was. I always wore a very small ruby and diamond cross on a gold chain that my parents gave me when I was young, and a gold and diamond K given to me by friends from childhood. Both were missing. I still did not realize I was in the hospital. Everyone laughed, cried, and was so happy that I was awake, had a memory, and was able to function well.

At that point I was told what happened. My last alive memory at that point had been in the kitchen at the house, as I shared earlier. Pieces started to be filled in by hospital staff, family and friends. My brothers were there. My brothers lived across the country in Chicago. Why were they there? I asked about my boy-friend. I was told he was not allowed to see me or talk to me. I was very confused.

I was informed by the doctors and nursing staff that I had been drugged and left to die. When the paramedics arrived, I was com-pletely unconscious and only an hour away from death. They told me that had I been left any longer I would have died. I fought off four paramedics as my blood adrenaline levels were crazy high. By this I mean that they were over fifty thousand; the average person's levels are between fifty and two hundred fifty. They had to sedate me and strap me down.

I thought I was given ecstasy. My blood panel showed I was given a cocktail mixture of seventeen different methamphetamines and roofies. My body temperature was over one hundred and six, and the hospital staff had put me in an ice bath and used charcoal to try and clear my system while I was still unconscious.

"You should be dead," said several doctors. "We have never seen something like this. It's miraculous. You are lucky to be alive." Those words would replay in my mind for many years.

I was in a haze and still very confused. Somehow I was aware that it was Monday, December 13. Somehow I had no organ damage at all, no brain damage, no signs of any kind of memory loss, aside from the time I was unconscious, and many pieces of that would come back over time.

The same day I woke up, a team of police officers and detectives came into my room. They asked me if I was willing to press charges against all the men who were in the house that night. They also told me that the family whose house I was at was part of a drug-running ring, bringing drugs from Mexico to Arizona, Colorado and Illinois.

I was still unclear mentally, and confused. They said if I pressed charges that they could finally catch these guys. They said I could press charges for attempted murder, as they'd left me to die. If I had died, they all would have been tried for murder. As far as I knew, no one else had any ill reaction to the drugs.

I asked if I could press charges against some of them, as I was trying to protect my boyfriend, but they said no. It was all or nothing. I chose not to do so. A part of me still wishes I had as a way of standing up for what was done to me. Even though I have walked a forgiveness journey, there are moments when I wonder what would have happened had I pressed charges.

Come to find out much later, this drug ring was orchestrated by Sammy Gravano, former mafioso and huge ecstasy ringleader, and the officers were seeking a way to put him in jail for good. If I had pressed charges, I would have been an integral part of that national investigation. I like to believe that God was protecting me by convincing me not to press charges.

When there was a quiet moment in the hospital room, I called my boyfriend at that house. This is when he shared with me his version of the story. He expressed his gratitude that I was alive, then told me that after they called 911, he'd called my parents to tell them what had happened. Once my parents and younger sister arrived at the hospital, Mom yelled at him and told him to leave. Understandable, and I am surprised that he was not beaten by my dad. My parents and younger sister were taken to the room in the ER that no parent ever wants to be taken.

I was dying. They told my parents not to expect me to make it. They told them that if I did make it I could be a vegetable. That my organs could shut down. That I may not remember them nor anyone else. I may be unable to think, talk, walk, et cetera. They said to prepare for the worst.

As a couple of days passed in the hospital, I was told I could not go home until my blood adrenaline levels came down to within range.

A social worker and counselor came to see me. They were worried I had a drug problem and needed therapy and perhaps even inpatient recovery. I explained that I had only done the drug one other time, that yes, I drank as most college students do, that I was a straight-A student, at least I was until that weekend, and I was not at risk for drug issues. Of all things, the effect on my grades was what I was angriest about. It's interesting to reflect back on this time and notice how distorted my mind was about what happened to me.

After a few days I was released from the ICU and transported by ambulance to the pediatric ward at another hospital. Though I was eighteen, they still were able to have me placed there, and said I would have better care. My brothers came and kept me company each day, watching movies and just hanging out. They told me that within minutes of receiving my parents' call they were on their way to the airport. My older sister was upset that she was not allowed to fly into town; she was in Michigan finishing her first semester finals for junior year of college.

The severity of what happened to me would not sink in for many years. On December 20, 1999, after a week in the hospital, I went home with no sign of any imbalance, organ issues, brain injuries, or aftereffects from the overdose that the doctors were expecting. Their words: "Kate, you are a walking miracle."

They told me that it was a ten-year window of time that I could have residual effects of the incident. I am still unsure of how they came up with ten years. Not one person talked with me about PTSD. Not one person mentioned mental health. Not one person asked if I had any history of prior trauma. No one.

I was able to take my finals after winter break, thanks to my best friend reaching out to every one of my professors to tell them what happened. I ended up with a 4.0 GPA that semester. The irony was not lost on me.

As I was trying to integrate into being human again, a part of my being was open to the other dimensions. It was a very strange time in my life. Both worlds were open to me. I saw spirits walking around in the world the same way I saw humans. I would wake up and see them in my bedroom. I would have dreams of being in both worlds. It was distorting and at times scary.

I worked with Kent to help me understand what had happened to me and why I was experiencing these things. I told him I didn't want to, and I was really scared by it all. Kent called me to his home, a place I'd visited many times.

We sat across from each other in the front living room – he on a black leather chair, me on a matching couch, a beautiful modern art coffee table between us. He proceeded to say these words to me: "Kate. Now that you have lived between worlds and have opened the door to the other realm, you must make a choice. You must choose whether you will walk in the Light and serve the Light, or well, you can infer the other option. I will no longer be able to assist you if you choose the other.

Just like in Star Wars, we each come to a point in our lives where we have to decide which path to choose, which side to serve. While the dark and shadows will always be there, when you choose to walk in the Light, as the Light, with the Highest Light, the dark may try, yet will always lose. When you come to know your darkness and choose your light, the dark will no longer have power over you. You know what this means, Kate. Choose wisely."

I chose the Light that day. Kent helped me focus the energy to show up only in dreams and not in daily life. This worked for about seven years. Once I had Connor, everything started opening up again. Since 2006, the human world and spirit world are one.

Three years after the overdose I was in Dad's home office and saw a post-it note on his desk. He was writing his book and occasionally there would be notes for him to remember something to add to it. This note said, "Kate. Died twice that day in the hospital."

I stopped in my tracks and stared at the note. This was the first time I ever heard of this. No one had told me I died. No one shared this part of my story – a rather important part, I would say. Angry and confused, I asked Dad what that note was about.

He shared with me that when I was rushed back into the ER, the doctors did not give me much chance of surviving. He called Kent, who met my parents and sister at the hospital. Kent also called his team of healers around the world to start working on me.

Dad also told me that when he saw my body, I was lifeless and a shallow resemblance of his often stubborn, lively daughter. My heart was struggling as I listened to Dad say that I died twice on the table that day. The doctors and nurses tried to resuscitate me, shocking me with a defibrillator, and my heart stopped. Time of death was called.

My parents were told there was nothing more that could be done. I was dead. My mom and sister were escorted to a waiting room alone, in shock and horror that I was gone.

Dad told the doctor that he had someone who could possibly help me, someone with other ways of healing. The doctor said that his grandmother had been a medicine woman of her own right, then something along the lines of, "We have done everything we can to save your daughter. Her heart has stopped. Let me remind you that your daughter is dead. You can bring in whomever you need to. There is nothing more we can do for her."

At that point Kent came back into the ER and he and Dad performed a shamanic ceremony over me. My dad prayed to Jesus and Mother Mary to save me. Kent was using his rattle and ancient ways to try and bring me back. Both went into a deep meditative journey to try and find me between worlds. Meanwhile, my mom and sister were still in the waiting room, believing that I was dead.

Miraculously, my heart started beating again, and doctors and nurses swarmed over my body. I did not stay alive long. Dad ran out to tell Mom and my sister of the miracle of me coming back to life, only to be interrupted moments later by a code calling – I was flatlining again. My heart stopped for a second time. More paddling, more shocking my body. Nothing.

I had died again. Time of death was called again. Kent was still in a channel, working on me. Dad shared that the doctor was in tears, sweating and apologizing, head hanging low. The rest of the staff were exhausted and grief-stricken.

This is what I remember from between worlds:

I first noticed something was wrong when I saw my body lifeless on the bed in a home I did not recognize. My boyfriend was there. I couldn't control my body. I was seizing and no one was helping me. I felt helpless and could not save myself. Why wasn't anyone helping me? Why was I unconscious? Why couldn't I wake up?

My body was not my own at that point. I remember being sexually assaulted that night by several men. I even remember the feeling of a knife, and I will be honest in saying that I didn't go any further into needing to know what happened. My body felt it and that is enough. My unconscious body was being used for their pleasure. I questioned myself over and over again on this, and the memories in my body kept speaking Truth.

I remember the feeling of being strapped down and restrained. I would come to find out that was due to firefighters and EMTs having to do so in order to get me to calm down. Even though I was unconscious, I was fighting them off me.

The next thing I remember is seeing myself lying on the hospital bed in the ER. I was not recognizable as me. I didn't want to come back into my body. My body hurt. Being human hurt. I didn't want to have to experience more pain, more trauma. My body remembered the sexual abuse, even though I consciously didn't. My body remembered the rape on prom night. My body remembered all the emotional pain and it was just too much. My body was struggling to stay alive and my soul was ready to call it quits. My spirit was ready to be free. Being human hurt and I wanted to be done.

I left the hospital and ascended into another realm. I saw a large golden room with a dome-like ceiling and a very long, dark mahogany table and twelve chairs. It looked like a beautiful temple. I was off to one side of the room sitting on the floor in a corner. The room had floor-to-ceiling bookshelves on one side and jeweled walls on the other. I remember the walls being so beautiful, layered in rubies, emeralds, sapphires, and amethyst, all bonded by gold. It was so incredible I still don't have the words to describe its ornate beauty.

There was a large pedestal with an old book opened on it in front of an altar with three other books. I would later come to see the title of three of the books: *The Book of Loss; The Book of*

Beauty"; and *The Book of Wisdom*. I still don't recall the title of the fourth book.

I would end up revisiting this room many times in dreams and in meditations, not knowing where I was, yet knowing I had been there before and feeling very comfortable whenever I was in the room. It was in this very room that I would offer forgiveness in 2018 to the people who'd harmed me throughout my life. I still visit this temple often in meditation and communion with God.

As I traveled between realms, I heard talking but I was unsure who was there. There was discussion over what had happened to me. They were saying that I did not choose to take the drug. That I actually *was* drugged, and that what I thought I was taking was not what I was given.

I heard them talking about if I died, whether I would go to a deeper soul review or to heaven. From what I remember, any time there is an intentional overdose or suicide, the soul goes to a review phase for healing. They don't go to "hell" as some religions will say. There is only love on the other side of the veil.

I remember seeing Jesus, some loved ones who had passed and higher beings. I remember hearing Mother Mary, although at that time I didn't give her much attention. You see, I associated her with my grandfather as he used to make me sit in his lap and say the rosary with him. He would tickle me and hold me so tight on his lap I couldn't escape. Through that association, any time I saw her, it made my whole body cringe.

That changed as I learned how much she'd helped me recover and heal through my life. In between worlds she appeared as White Buffalo Calf Woman, knowing if she said Mother Mary I would shut her out.

While in this jeweled temple I talked with her. I recall walking up to the table, saying, "I don't want to hurt anymore. I don't want to keep being in pain. It was too hard to be human. I want to stay here."

She told me that the worst was over, that I would have much healing to do on my soul, but that my life would get better and be beautiful. I recall her telling me my time was not done yet. I had more to do on Earth. I remember her saying to me that I needed to return, but it was my choice.

I said, "Okay," committing to returning to my body, yet not really wanting to do so.

I remember her touching my heart. I remember the feeling of her hands pressing firmly into my heart space right at my sternum while she said in a loud, commanding tone, over all the other people present, "She's not done yet!"

This is the last thing I remember about being between worlds. The words of Mother Mary, as White Buffalo Calf Woman: "She's not done yet."

I often found my hands on my sternum when feeling anxious or overwhelmed. It is an unconscious thing. Little did I know it is a pattern of calming my body and mind and helping me to stay grounded in my body in times when I want to dissociate.

My heart started beating again. Dad would later tell me that my right hand grabbed Kent's twirling pendulum over my solar plexus, yet I had not fully awoken. Doctors and nurses swarmed around me, pushing Dad and Kent out of the way, hooking me back up to all the machines. They were in awe and amazement at what they had just witnessed and did not understand.

When I shared with Dad my experiences in this temple, his eyes welled up. He asked if I knew where I was. I didn't. He had seen the same temple during the ceremony over my body. He was in there and so was Kent. They both saw it. Dad also has memories of Mother Mary being there too.

December 12, 1999. That is my rebirth date. The day my heart started again. The day I chose to live. It is also the day of Our Lady of Guadalupe, the day of honoring Mother Mary. There are no coincidences in life. This I know as Truth.

In 2012, while I was in my first yoga therapy training, Mother Mary presented herself to me again as White Buffalo Calf Woman, helping me to begin the embodiment phase of my healing journey.

Over the years and through a lot of EMDR and yoga therapy, I have remembered and put together pieces of what I was experiencing during this time between worlds. Fragments of images that had flashed in my mind for seventeen years finally started coming together.

Dad hadn't told me because he didn't want me to remember things I wasn't ready to face. Kent and others involved in the ceremony also didn't tell me. I understand that now, even though at the time I was very hurt. I know I wasn't ready to handle the truth of what had happened to me. I would often ask Kent to help me remember what happened. He would respond by saying that some things are better off not being remembered until it is time.

For many years my body would have memories of being paddled to try and restart my heart. My heart would jump and skip beats. My chest would ache and thump as if they were paddling me at that moment. This was before I knew that they had done this to me many times.

This was before I was told that I died.

It frequently happened while I was sleeping at night. My heart would stop and I would jolt up and hear the words, "Clear!" In fact, those words used to be a trigger for me and I did not understand why.

After the overdose, I vowed not to use another illegal drug ever again. I was also very scared of using any kind of medication, this being one of the reasons I was resistant to taking the Xanax. I was not sure what it would do to me, especially since I'd had reactions to several other pharmaceutical and over-the-counter medications over the years.

After sharing a very short version of this story with my doctor, she still insisted that I try it. She said, "All the cows are out of the barn, and you need to get them back inside." No compassion to the story, no wondering about the long-term effects on my health, no questions or validations of how this experience alone could be causing a lot of the mental health symptoms I was suffering with so deeply each day. Instead, she offered only a very odd metaphor to try to explain that the pieces of me I had not healed and integrated were taking over my psychological well-being. Her answer was drugs. I lost trust in her that day.

CHAPTER ELEVEN

MOTHER MARY RETURNS

My doctor continued her regular standard of care, and when I saw her in July 2016 complaining of headaches and neck pain she ordered an MRI of my brain to see what was going on. I think she was mostly trying to appease me. The last time I had an MRI was years prior when my previous doctor thought I had MS due to numbness and tingling in my left arm, dizziness, headaches. The MRI was clear. It was a reaction to an IUD I had implanted after having my daughter. My body rejected it. I believe my body was always trying to find a way to get me to resolve these traumas.

The level of anxiety I had about going for the MRI was intense, but I was determined to do it without medication. Since 2009 I have practiced yoga nidra,[5] a mindfulness-based meditation practice during which the brainwaves move from the beta state, where they are during normal, active hours, into the delta – or deep sleep-like – state (in fact "nidra" is the Sanskrit word for sleep), where profound healing occurs. Then, through intentional placement of empowering statements, the old, unhealthy patterns are replaced with new, positive programming. This practice has been studied extensively and is proven to help in recovery from trauma, reducing the stress response, and reversing the long-term effects of both.

As a dedicated practitioner and teacher of this work, I was confident that if I could just get myself into that state during the MRI, I would be okay.

I scheduled the MRI very early in the morning so I could wake up, go and come home to rest. Eric was going with me, and he was hoping I would take a pill to calm down. I told him I would be fine. Even though I still had lots of anxiety, I also felt a sense of peace. It was going to be okay.

When I got onto the sliding table to go into the MRI machine, the tech asked me if there was anything I needed to be more comfortable. I asked him if he had any extra blankets to place over my feet and stomach to help keep me calm. He looked at me a little sideways and said that he had some sand-bags. "Perfect!" I exclaimed. He laughed. "Really?" "Yes! That is perfect. Please place one on my feet and one on my lower stomach."

He did. "So this really helps, huh?"

"Yes. It calms the nervous system."

"Good to know. I can offer this to other patients who struggle with anxiety here. What kind of music do you want to listen to? We use Pandora so I can put on anything."

"There is a station called Reiki Meditation music. Could you please put that on?"

"Sure."

He slid the table into the larger bore MRI, as I'd requested when scheduling the appointment. I was covered from head to torso, and I had to have one of those cradles over my head, keeping my head and neck still. In the past, this head cradle sent me spinning. I was grateful that did not happen this time. The music came on and it was what I requested.

The test started and the thumping and knocking of the MRI was somewhat drowned out by the melody of the Reiki music. I took a few deep breaths and imagined being guided into my body as if in a yoga nidra. I heard my teacher's voice in my mind, taking me through the practice.

I am not sure how far into the MRI I was (the total exam was an hour), but I saw this glowing iridescent light all around me. This color brought me so much comfort. A lavender violet, white light emanating peacefulness. I can still see it now. Just heavenly.

I drifted off deep into meditation, yet was fully aware of my body and of being in an MRI machine. I felt someone behind me holding me, as if I was resting back into the most loving arms imaginable. I heard her say, "Shhh...you are going to be okay. Just rest, sweet child. I am here." I knew right away it was Mother Mary holding me. I felt her warmth, her love, her comfort, and her grace. A few years prior she had reintroduced herself as Mother Mary in a meditation. She called me, "Sweet Child." This would become her term of endearment when she was wanting my attention.

As she held me, she spoke to me. "You are going to feel some things being pulled out of you. There are some darker energies inside you that I need to take out. Just rest and let them do what they need to do to remove them."

I felt two other presences at my feet. Huge energies, very strong, and protective. As I laid back into her arms, everything in my body relaxed. Deep peace overcame me. I felt dark cords being pulled out of my feet, as if someone was pulling an electrical cord out from being tied in a knot. It felt like it was being pulled from all the way up in my abdomen.

I was covered in chills as energy was moving so quickly through me. The color of the light was so pure and healing. I still wish I could recreate it. Nothing quite matches it to this day. I rested deeply into this experience of peace, and Divine appointment.

The MRI machine stopped.

"You will be okay. Trust that all will be okay. I love you. You are so deeply loved. Remember that, Kate." She spoke these words into my ear as the music stopped.

The table pulled me out of the machine. I felt so peaceful, more so than in many months.

The tech said, "Well, I guess the music and sandbags really work. You were so still we didn't have to redo any of the imaging at all. That rarely happens."

"Yep. I feel great," I said, smiling inside.

When I walked back into the waiting room, Eric could tell something had happened. As we got to the car, I started sharing with him this incredible experience.

He smiled. "Only you, Kate," he said in his endearing voice and with soft, blue eyes.

I left that appointment hopeful and calm, clinging to her promises that I would be okay.

CHAPTER TWELVE

MY MIND BECAME
MY WORST ENEMY

It was a Thursday night shortly after the MRI. Don't know why I remember it being a Thursday night, yet I do. I was sitting down at the kitchen table about to eat dinner with my family. It had not been a very hard day that I recall, just the usual anxiety and shaking as I tried to see clients. The peacefulness I'd felt during the MRI had faded quickly. As I sat down, I looked to my right and saw the steak knife next to my plate.

"You should use that to hurt yourself, Kate. Just stop the pain already." It was as if the knife was speaking to me.

I froze. The voice in my head was my own voice. I was not hearing another voice. It was a part of me that I believe I had shut out for many years and was finally tired of being pushed away. I was beyond scared. I had never in my life prior to that moment thought of hurting myself. Even when I was struggling with postpartum depression after the birth of my son, I did not think those thoughts. I had what I know to be other intrusive thoughts, but I did not have suicidal thoughts. I ate dinner, got up from the table, went into my room and cried. What was happening to me? Why was this happening?

The days and weeks that followed were a spiral of darkness. My doctor didn't know what to do for me. She knew I was seeing my therapist and kept pushing the Xanax. The MRI came back clear, as I knew it would.

I used every practice imaginable that I knew how to do: yoga, meditation, journaling. I learned Emotional Freedom Technique,[6] EFT, a form of therapy that works with lightly tapping on meridian points in the body to open up blocked energy, and tapped every day, multiple times. I would go on long walks outside, sitting in the grass, crying and not understanding why I was so sad and feeling so destroyed inside. None of my tools were working. I felt like everything I had learned over the past twenty years was broken.

Most nights I would hide in my bedroom, taking a bath, trying to calm the shaking, and journal. Often I would end up on the floor in my closet, my cat would join me, and I would put my body in a ball and cry, shaking, pleading with God to end this pain.

I had completely lost my ability to be a mom. I was not able to show up for my kids or husband. I could barely function. I was canceling with clients, subbing out my classes and my thoughts were getting worse and worse each day.

Gratefully, I had the awareness that they were just thoughts, not truths, and my therapist was helpful in giving me reminders of this. Just parts of me were scared of what I was feeling. She was also great at providing cognitive behavioral therapy (CBT), but she did not have the skills to help me process and integrate the various traumas.

On Sunday, August 21, 2016, Eric was out of town and I was home alone with my kids. I was not okay, and as I sat to have breakfast I felt myself falling fast. To describe it is rather difficult. I felt like the floor was falling out from under me. I couldn't ground into my body. I felt totally dissociative and dizzy.

I called Makena, then seven years old, to come over to me.

"Makena. Please call Titi Michelle on my phone. Ask her if she can come over. Tell her I am not okay and I need help."

Makena left my younger sister a message.

I went to take a bath to try and ground. As I was laying in the tub, I went into a meditation. I saw myself buried underground. I heard the voices of my healers who had died years prior. They were telling me that I was being rebirthed. That all this pain was purposeful and I would understand it sooner than later. That I would know why I had to go through everything I had from such a young age and now this. They told me to trust.

I came out of the meditation to find my sister at my house. She was scared. I called my therapist. She asked me if I wanted to hurt myself.

"No, I don't. I just can't ground and I can't get my mind to be okay. What is wrong with me? Why can't I function? I feel like the ground is going to fall out from me."

"Kate, come see me tomorrow. Call Eric and tell him to come home. You need him home. You don't need to go to the hospital unless you feel you are at risk of hurting yourself. You are telling me you don't want to do that, so let's see you tomorrow. Look at your joy journal and do some of those things on that list."

Months prior, she had asked me what brought me joy. I had no idea. She said to just pay attention to the things in my life that made me smile, light up inside, and laugh. That's when I realized I didn't feel joy. I lived in anger, fear, sadness, resent, mixed with a few moments of happiness throughout my day. Gratitude was a practice, yet felt forced, not real and true.

I spent a lot of time seeking out joy. I started a joy journal and would list out the things that opened my heart. I recall being at a grocery store after that therapy session where she asked me about joy. I was standing in the coffee aisle trying to decide on what coffee to buy. A seemingly easy decision, yet I was not capable of making choices at that time. Making decisions was a trigger for me. Shame controlled my every thought and decision, as if choosing the wrong coffee would cost me all the love in my life. I was so irrational and had no idea how to recover a sound mind.

A little boy, maybe three years of age, was in the cart next to me; his mom also looking at coffee. He looked right into my eyes, smiled, said hi and laughed. He was playing with a toy and in such joy. I felt my mouth smile for the first time in a while. I felt my heart open up just a bit.

I thought to myself, "Oh, this is joy. It's found in the small moments. It doesn't have to be a big Hollywood effect. It's in the simple things too."

I walked out of that store with a newfound mission to reclaim my joy. I didn't know how I was going to do it, but it was what I needed. I needed to feel hopeful again.

I called my husband and told him what was happening to me. He asked me if I needed to go to the hospital. I told him I'd talked with my therapist and what she said.

He was home within a few hours, terrified at what was happening to his once very strong, capable wife. I was very thin and completely depleted of all energy and life in my body. I felt like I was dying inside and couldn't find my way out of this darkness. I felt see-through. My energy was gone. I had nothing left to give. When he got home, I crawled in bed and cried, shaking myself to sleep.

CHAPTER THIRTEEN

RECONNECTING TO THE LIGHT OF CHRIST

On August 22, during a session with my therapist, I told her what happened in the bathtub. She was excited. Her shaman side came out and she gave me some insights into ceremonial rebirth according to shamanic tradition. I left there that day with my thoughts a little more settled.

As soon as I walked in my home, however, I felt this sinking feeling in my stomach. I stood in the middle of my living room floor, the ground shaking, the room starting to spin, my thoughts beginning to spiral again. I instantly fell to my knees with a force. A cathartic cry came out of my mouth, as tears began to pour down my eyes.

"Jesus, please help me. God, please help me. I can't do this on my own anymore. What the fuck is wrong with me? What is happening?" I screamed. I cried. I pounded my fists on the ground. My body was moving in and out of prostrations as I cried. I just wanted this pain to end.

I felt a warm hand on my upper back. It was a feeling I'd had one other time in my life. When I was fifteen, I had to have ACL reconstructive surgery on my left knee due to a basketball injury. The night before, I was sleeping, trying to at least, and feeling anxious over having surgery the next morning. Suddenly, I'd felt this warm hand press on my upper back. It was a comforting feeling, heavy, grounding, and filled with love. I felt someone sitting on my bed by my side. I felt this presence of safety and love all night.

While on my living room floor crying and screaming, that same feeling overcame me. Instant safety, grounding, heaviness, love filled my being. I felt a presence kneeling next to me. I felt as if I could lean into it, knowing I was being supported.

I heard the words, "Surrender it to me. Surrender into my grace, Kate. You don't have to do this on your own. I am here with you. I have always been here with you. You have never been alone. I have always carried you through those moments of terror. I have been by your side through it all and I will carry you through this too. Trust me. Remember your faith."

I recognized the voice and the feeling. It was Jesus. He was with me as a child, he was with me in the hospital. He was with me between worlds. He was with me after the overdose as I found my way into the light.

For the first time in months, all the shaking inside my body stopped. There was a calm inside my body. A new kind of calm. I felt a renewed sense of being. I stood up in gratitude. Things settled down for a few days.

I found a new love of Christian radio and started listening regularly. I started reading a daily devotional that focused on the Joy of Jesus. I prayed often and journaled to Him each day. My favorite song at that time was Lion and the Lamb by Big Daddy Weave. Whenever I heard that song, I felt the spirit move through me. It had an empowering, comforting effect on my nervous system.

I found some strength and was able to help make meals for my kids again. I could handle watching a movie and didn't need to cancel clients. My body was still shaking fairly regularly, and the anxiety would come in waves, but the nightmares stopped and I was able to get some good sleep. I felt like I was finally on the road to healing. I kept seeing my therapist and she was excited about my shifts.

A couple of weeks later, I fell back into despair and depression. I don't know what caused it. I reached out to one of my mentors, the teacher I had learned yoga nidra from and had been studying with for five years at that point. I told her that I couldn't do yoga nidra. It wasn't working. I told her that it was as if someone had taken away the access to peace and I was floundering.

I was crying in my closet again, wishing that I could find that moment of peace. She emailed me back fairly quickly, telling me to stop practicing yoga nidra. She said she could feel what I was going through and yoga nidra was not the right practice at that time for me.

She reminded me of a practice called energetic diffusion technique (EDT), a practice I'd learned many years prior and taught often to others. When you are in a trauma response, the brain has a hard time remembering what to do to help bring balance. EDT, which is part of the process described in the water metaphor in Chapter 4, allows energy to move through the body without trying to control it or change it. It is a practice of surrender, compassion, and grace. EDT helps you learn how to allow sensations to be present without taking you over. She suggested I do this practice instead as often as I needed to clear and move this energy. She reminded me of some of the deeper teachings about energy and that I was experiencing a blockage trying to move. Instead of allowing it to move, I was resisting it. The resistance was causing more suffering than feeling it through.

The lyrics of The Beatles song "Let It Be" played in my mind. Stop resisting what is, listen to the wisdom of Mother Mary, and it would release faster.

I already had the recording of the process on my phone. I listened to it five times in a row that night. After the fifth time, the shaking stopped and I could finally think straight. Deep down inside I knew something was unwell and yet my doctor and therapist were confident I was on the right track to healing.

Eric and I had been talking more about needing to get back to our faith. We lived across the street from a large church but had never attended. I was not interested in religion, having grown up Catholic then pulled away as my family became more metaphysical in my teenage years; also, the grandfather who'd abused me had been a "man of faith." Eric grew up a nondenominational Christian, the same as the church by us. I knew some friends and clients who also went to this church and really enjoyed it.

A fellow yoga teacher and friend said that the church was much more about a relationship with Jesus than a religion. She recently switched to that church as they were more accepting and open, more community-based, than her previous church.

We chose to start going on a Saturday night in mid-September. My physical body was still shaking and exhausted. I was in a constant state of hypervigilance and unable to bring my nervous system into complete calm.

We checked the kids into the children's service and walked into the large church auditorium. I could hear music playing from outside. I had no idea what to expect, and was unaware that they played modern Christian music as worship at the beginning of service. My experiences at church were hymns and choir music.

When we walked inside, the song "Lion and the Lamb" was being played by the band. I was overcome with Spirit and almost fell to my knees. Eric had to hold me up. The feeling of complete love and peace moving through my body was so intense I could barely walk. Tears were pouring down my cheeks. We walked up the steps to find a seat in the stadium seating area, as lower seats were filled. This was the biggest church I had ever been in and by far the most worship energy I had ever felt. I felt at home. I shook through the entire service. Eric tried to comfort me and calm my body. Tears kept coming down.

I was reminded of the safe feeling I would get when I went to church as a young child. While I never connected to the dogma of religion, the sacred rituals of mass always moved Spirit through me, even as a little girl.

We started going to church each week as a family, enjoying the time together and the peacefulness it would bring to my soul. I felt safe there, and immersed in Spirit, crying throughout every service.

I know now that my body was unwinding all this time, and my nervous system was shaking out all the trauma that had been living inside it for so many years. My constant state of fear and not being able to process out the decades of pain were released through shaking and tears.

I remembered reading *Waking the Tiger*[7] in my first yoga therapy training in 2012. Dr. Peter Levine talks about how our nervous system will start to shake to release the trauma and shock after an experience that is intense, just like an animal in the wild after getting away from a predator. The difference is an animal doesn't have the ego-mind that we have to stop the shaking. They will let it shake until the entire system is rebalanced. Our mind will try to stop the release, make sense of it, control it, numb it, repress it, avoid it. The only way to allow the trauma to release is to let it be, and feel it through.

This is what was happening to me, although I was not doing a good job of feeling it through, and trying hard to manage it, control it, stop it.

Towards the end of September I went back to the doctor. She had run some blood work and saliva samples to check my adrenal function and hormones again. She upped my level of progesterone and was having me take adrenal supplements, as my reports were not good. Cortisol was pumping through me way too fast, and my adrenals were burning out. I was exhausted and still very anxious. She had me continue with the Xanax as needed, although I still had not finished one prescription, which she was upset about. She said I was not using it enough.

I was kind of a medical mystery to her, and while I appreciated her efforts to solve it, I feel she was in over her head with me, and didn't know what to do.

My therapist, in the meantime, was beginning to get frustrated that I was still struggling so much. She kept telling me it was all about shifting my thoughts. I told her I was well aware of my thoughts and how to change them. I told her that even though I could think healthy thoughts, the distorted thoughts kept coming through. Her suggestions were to not give them my time and energy.

If only it was that easy. It wasn't. I felt ashamed that I could not do as she asked, yet I also knew that she did not understand how the body talks or how to use it in therapy. Her messages became shaming and triggering.

I began praying to God to lead me to a therapist who better understood how to use the body in therapy. I also needed someone who was on our insurance as paying out of pocket each week was hurting us financially. Somehow I kept finding the inner strength to keep going each day, even if just a few minutes at a time, knowing that I did not go through all that past pain to live life in such despair.

CHAPTER FOURTEEN

TRAUMA THERAPY BEGINS

I knew I needed someone who offered EMDR with a body-centered approach. I was familiar with EMDR as several clients had used it in their own healing, but I had yet to experience this therapy myself. Now I was ready to move forward.

I researched local therapy practices, hoping that I could find someone who took health insurance, and found one twenty minutes from my home. When I called, I asked the scheduler for a therapist who specializes in trauma, EMDR, and who was spiritually open. This was a big step. I was scared that if someone knew about my spiritual life, they would instantly want to send me to a mental hospital.

I was given the name of a therapist and an appointment later that week. When I arrived at my new therapist's office, it was cold, very medical, and I was unsure of how this was going to go. A woman came out of a therapy room; of medium stature, she had black and blonde hair and was wearing a long black cloak, an owl shirt, and black boots. She had a soft smile but a tough demeanor. Her laugh was loud and fun, her voice kind.

"Hi, Kate. I'm Paula. Come with me."

I followed her into a small room with a hard, modern grey loveseat, two end tables, a brown desk, and a chair across from the couch. The air was cold, and the lighting harsh.

I don't recall what she asked me. I started telling my story. I was careful not to divulge too much about my energetic side, as I was unsure what she would be okay with. I was still in fear of being sent to the hospital.

Paula asked me a series of questions relating to PTSD. She said I would be a good candidate for EMDR due to my traumatic past, and was fairly upset that my previous therapist didn't suggest I do more specific trauma therapy. I was happy to hear this. I knew EMDR worked, and I knew that I was not receiving the healing I needed from cognitive behavioral therapy.

Then Paula asked me what my spiritual beliefs were. I paused. Do I tell her that I have done psychic work and mediumship for years? Do I tell her that I talk with spirits, angels, loved ones? Do I tell her that I can see energy move, and where it is blocked in people's bodies? Do I tell her that I can see spirits sometimes? Do I tell her that people shapeshift in front of me and I am aware of the imbalances they are suffering from, often before they are? Do I tell her about my death experience?

Instead, I told her that I believe in Jesus, Mother Mary, Archangels. That I am very open spiritually and need someone who can understand this part of me.

She smiled and laughed. She said that her friends call her "the crazy owl lady." She said we would get along just fine. I felt my whole body relax. We planned to meet weekly.

When I saw her next, we did more intake and I told her pieces of what had happened earlier that year. Paula was taking the time to build trust and rapport, essential steps in feeling safe to work with her. I was often still dissociative, finding it very difficult to stay present in my body. I explained all the various practices I had done and was doing to help myself heal. She told me she would not do any EMDR with me until I stopped everything but yoga, meditation, journaling. She said I was dipping in too many wells and my system was getting confused about what I was asking it to do at this time. I agreed to stop the other practices.

It was early October 2016, and I finally felt like someone understood me. Paula helped me to understand how EMDR was going to work, how it may feel like I am in two places at once, as it taps into the subconscious mind in the present moment. She said that it could cover more healing in one session than years of talk therapy. I felt hopeful. I knew talking about all the pain was not helping to heal the wounds.

Feeling I needed more integrative and holistic care I called a naturopathic doctor and got an appointment in a few weeks' time. My general practitioner was not helping, and she was getting frustrated with me as well. She even said to me at one appointment, "Every time I know I'm going to see you, I get ungrounded and nervous. Your anxiety is just too much. I'm not sure what else to do for you."

She then wrote me a referral for an endocrinologist and a prescription for Zoloft, an antidepressant. Finally, she suggested I see a psychiatrist.

I called the endocrinologist and took the first appointment I could get, five weeks out. Still reluctant to take medication, I researched Zoloft, also known as sertraline, and found many had success using it. She didn't have a referral for a psychiatrist and said to google one. I called a few psychiatrists' offices and no one could get me in for six to eight weeks. I scheduled with one of the doctors at the end of November.

Desperate to feel well, I caved and started the medication on Wednesday, October 19, 2016. By Thursday evening, I was not okay. The shaking was worse, I was so nauseous, and couldn't think straight. I was supposed to go to Sedona, where a friend and I were co-leading a retreat from Friday afternoon through Sunday. Unsure if I could do it, I called my friend and told her what was happening. She was okay with playing it by ear, and perfectly capable of holding it on her own if needed.

At this time I was also very aware that my family needed the money I would earn from the retreat. My medical bills had put us into major debt and I was not able to work as much, making things very difficult financially. The financial pressure and inner turmoil was causing me to feel like things were collapsing again, and I was losing the little bit of hope I had gained.

Friday morning I woke up feeling sick. I was vomiting up what looked like bile, and my mind was not well. I couldn't find any clear thoughts, and was not sure if I could find the strength to go to Sedona. I took a Xanax to calm the anxiety and try to make sense of what was happening.

After a few hours of self-care, I made the decision to head up for the retreat. The entire weekend I was in and out of dissociation, sweating, not able to sleep unless I took Xanax. My friend helped me through it all and was a Godsend of support as we led twelve women through an inward journey of self-discovery and empowerment, while I was just barely making it through each day.

I shared with the retreat attendees about what was happening to me. They were very gracious, telling me how vulnerable and empowering they found it that I was being so honest and raw in a very delicate time. In hindsight, I was not in a place to lead anything. I was not in my right mind, and believe me, I had to process this experience in therapy too. By the end of the retreat I could barely function. I had a migraine, was unable to think clearly, and the intrusive thoughts had returned, only this time even worse. I didn't make the connection that it could be from the medication.

I needed to be home the following morning for a medical appointment, yet was not in any condition to drive down the mountain by myself late at night. I chose to stay at my friend's home, as she lived just up the road from the retreat center. She set me up on her futon for the night. I tried to fall asleep without medication and found myself shaking and sweating again, my mind racing uncontrollably. Breath work was not helping and I felt desperate to feel some relief. I took half a Xanax, just to try to calm down. As sensitive as I am to medication, a half pill has the same effect as a full one for most people.

I fell into a semi-sleep state, then was abruptly woken up by a man's voice saying, "Hi. I am Sam." I jolted awake and looked around but saw no one. This was not a real person, I realized, but a spirit speaking to me. I had never had it happen like this before. Whenever I heard Spirit, it was more of an inner voice, not as if someone was next to me talking!

I knew I had crossed a line mentally and was not in a good place. My friend was sleeping and I didn't want to wake her and alarm her. I waited a couple of hours, shaking in fear now, as I had no idea what was happening to my mind, just that it was in a bad state. After trying unsuccessfully to fall back to sleep, I decided to head down to Phoenix earlier than planned.

As I was driving down the winding mountain roads of the I-17, I kept my mind in prayer, and on the Christian radio playing loudly in my car. It was all I could do to keep my eyes open and focused on driving. Intrusive thoughts were coming in about just driving off the mountain road, life not being worth living if this is how I was going to feel, then about how that would hurt my kids and Eric...it went on and on.

When I got home I was a mess. The panic attacks would not end, and I was so grateful I was seeing Paula that afternoon. When I walked in she took one look at me and said, "Kate. What is going on? You are shaking even worse, your skin is red, your eyes are bloodshot, you are sweating and your heart rate is up."

"I started taking Zoloft last week by order of my doctor. She said I needed to be on an antidepressant. I have felt unwell since. My mind has been worse, much worse, too."

"Kate, you need to go to the hospital. I have seen many people on Zoloft and they do not look like this. I think you are having an allergic reaction to the medication."

She called Eric, and he and the kids came right over to get me. Paula explained what she thought was happening and said he needed to get me to the ER. If he couldn't, she would take me.

When we got to the hospital my anxiety was moving towards panic attacks. Makena and Connor were scared, and I was just trying to hold it together for them. Lots of prayers in my head as I waited to be taken back. Eric called my in-laws to come and get my kids. This was the second time they'd seen me taken to the ER due to anxiety. The first time, a couple of years prior, I thought I was having gallbladder pain.

When I went back into the ER exam room, the doctor agreed that I was having an allergic reaction to the Zoloft, which from what he said is quite rare. No surprise, as I am usually an anomaly.

He said I needed to stop taking it immediately. He also gave me an Ativan, which like Xanax is a benzodiazepine but not as addictive. They didn't give Xanax at the hospital, he explained, because it is so highly addictive and only has a four-hour life in the body. When I told him what my doctor had been doing, he was not surprised and disagreed with the way she had been telling me to use Xanax for the past ten months. I am thankful I listened to my intuition and not my doctor. The ER doc said to call my doctor in the morning but to see a psychiatrist, not her, for meds. You wouldn't see your general practitioner for cancer. Mental health is just as serious.

I went home feeling defeated yet relieved that it was the medication causing the increase in symptoms. The next morning, Tuesday, I called my doctor to tell her what happened and what the ER doctor had said about Zoloft and Xanax. She said, "Just go see that endocrinologist I referred you to and schedule with a psych. You can go back on the herbal supplement to help with the anxiety. Stop taking the Zoloft, Xanax, and all your hormones. It is obviously not working."

"You want me to stop all the meds and hormones?" I asked. The last time I had taken the Zoloft was Sunday night, and though the ER doc had told me to stop taking it immediately I wanted her confirmation. "Do you want me to follow up with you?"

"Yes. Do not contact me until after you see a psychiatrist."

"Okay."

I listened to what she told me to do. Cold-turkey stopped the Zoloft, all Xanax, and the hormones. I had no idea what this could do to someone's system. Wednesday morning I woke up and knew I had lost my mind.

"Kate, just do it already," I thought. "Kill yourself. You don't really want to be here anymore. You can't handle this life. See, even your doctor doesn't know what to do with you. You are a problem, a burden. Your family will be better off without you. Why don't you just do it already?"

I called a friend and told her I was not okay. She talked with me for a bit and helped me to calm down. It was six-thirty am.

Though I no longer co-owned the yoga studio I was still teaching there. I called my previous business partners and told them I needed subs for my classes that morning. There was no way I could teach.

My husband got my kids off to school and I went outside to sit in the sun. I would often sit on my front patio and drink my coffee and allow nature to help ground me. Usually it helped quite a bit.

It didn't that day. By ten a.m. I was deeply worried about my mind. It was an interesting place to be. I was aware of my mind, my thoughts, and that I didn't want to hurt myself, and yet I couldn't control the thoughts trying to change my mind. The self-awareness I had was helping me to know that I was not okay. I was very blessed to have all the years of training in holistic therapies helping me during this time, yet it still was not enough to combat whatever was happening in my psyche and soul.

I called another friend who was aware of what I had been going through.

"Do you want me to come over?"

"Yes, please. I'm scared."

"What are you afraid of?"

"I am afraid I may hurt myself."

"I am on my way."

About thirty minutes later she arrived with the friend I called earlier that morning. When they walked into my house, they both gave me a big hug and asked me to sit down.

"Kate, it's time to get some further help. This has gone on for too long and you are not getting any better. You need to see a psychiatrist or go to a hospital to get help."

I started to cry. I knew they were right. We all went to work researching psychiatrists, then I called three of them. The earliest appointment was still six weeks out.

The only other option was an in-patient mental/behavioral health hospital. I was familiar with a few of them around the Phoenix area, as I had been looking over the previous two weeks. Something in me must have known this was going to happen. There were only a few options that accepted my health insurance. The treatment center I wanted to go to was self-pay only, and we didn't have the forty-thousand dollars to get me admitted there.

One of my friends called my doctor's office on my behalf to ask if they had any other recommendations. They were not very kind to her, and she gave them an earful about poor medical care and what they did to my medication and possibly my mind by taking me off both an SSRI and all hormones at the same time.

I called my therapist and she recommended a couple places for me to look into. She was in agreement that I needed some additional care at this time. I called Eric to tell him what was going on. He came straight home from work very concerned and sad. He too knew it was the right decision.

We chose for me to go to a local hospital, the same one where I'd birthed both my children, and where I had gone two days prior for the allergic reaction to the medication. I figured at least they knew my medical history; perhaps they could help me and I could go home that night.

Eric arranged for Michelle to pick the kids up from school that afternoon. I went to shower while my friends packed a bag for me. They knew what I didn't know. I would be staying in the hospital.

While I was in the shower, my rational mind kicked back in. Water often did this to me. I felt fine. When I got out of the shower I was clear, and having second thoughts about going to the hospital.

My friends helped me understand that this is what happened to me. I would be rational and clear, and then all of a sudden I would be out of my right mind and as if I couldn't think straight. I would feel brain foggy, dizzy, confused and then the intrusive thoughts would kick in and make things worse.

I agreed to go to the hospital. They watched as I got in the car with Eric. I was silent at first, then started crying and apologizing for not being well. I felt so much shame that I couldn't get better, that I had been such a mess all year, that nothing was working, that we had spent all this money, that I couldn't work much, that I was not able to help take care of our kids much at all, that I had been hiding each night, barely getting by. I apologized through snot-filled tears, feeling completely broken, abandoned by God, and angry with Jesus – where was He in all of this? I felt angry at my past, pissed off at my body, very worried about my mind, and unsure that I would ever feel okay again.

Internally I agreed that I would do what the doctors at the hospital suggested, and I was hoping they would be able to get me in with a psychiatrist soon, very soon.

CHAPTER FIFTEEN

I FOUND GOD
IN A MENTAL HOSPITAL

I had to go in through the ER, as that is standard procedure for mental health concerns. They recognized me from a couple days before.

"Why are you back here?"

"I am scared I am going to hurt myself. I am having suicidal ideations."

I was immediately taken back to the exam room, where they had me undress and put on hospital scrubs. They took all my belongings and gave them to my husband. A doctor came in to see me and asked me a ton of questions. I don't remember most of them, but I know that with each one I felt more ashamed and broken.

"You will be taken back to a waiting area for our mental health ward of the hospital. I am not sure how long you will have to wait there. It gets busy. A nurse will see you and evaluate next steps."

I was escorted to a part of the hospital I had never seen before, a waiting room with many metal chairs, televisions, a few recliners, blankets. I was the only one there at that time, but within the next thirty minutes many other patients were brought in; some were taken into a room right away, while others waited with me. I was told there were no beds available in the mental health unit, as Arizona was very short on mental health help.

I figured I would be there for a few hours, seen by a psychiatrist, given a new medication to try, and sent home. A few hours went by and nothing. The nurses were taking other patients who they felt were at a higher risk, and seeing those who were coming in detoxing or very high on other medications.

I had Eric call my parents to let them know what was happening and where I was. While I knew they would freak out, I also wanted them to be aware of the seriousness of my internal suffering. Even at thirty-five years of age, I was still seeking my parents to show up for me in a way that helped me feel seen and understood. Shame is a deep, empty well of pain.

I would sit there for over twenty-four hours while other patients took priority. I spent that time praying, breathing, crying, in and out of rational thinking and going from emotionally drowning to complete numbness. My thoughts shifted to my kids. I decided at that moment that they were my "why." I may not have wanted to live in this pain anymore, but I refused to cause them the ultimate pain. I made an internal vow at that moment to fight for my life no matter how long it took. My kids deserved a mom who was happy, healthy, balanced, and able to be a safe, loving place for them to land.

Once I was called back for evaluation, I thought I would be put on a new med and sent home. When I got back to the evaluation room, the nurse's name was Angel. I smiled, silently thanking God.

Angel then informed me that I would be admitted for a minimum of five days. I lost it. Tears. Lots of tears. I recall asking why I couldn't just get meds and go home. He said they had to admit me, that since I was so sensitive to meds I needed to be overseen for a few days after starting the new medication. I looked at my husband and apologized. I felt so broken. So ashamed. He could barely meet my gaze.

I remember saying to him, "This is what I have to do."

I had to sleep in the "waiting in limbo area," as I call it, overnight because there were no beds for me yet. Michelle stayed with the kids so Eric could wait there with me.

When the next shift of nurses came on I had to laugh. My new nurse's name was Kent. God is always with us, I thought, a direct contrast to how I'd felt twenty-four hours prior. Little did I know that this hospital visit would be more of a spiritual journey than I ever could have imagined.

I was checked in and my husband had to leave. Before clocking out Angel had promised that he would make sure my roommate was someone with similar symptoms, and he did. Her name was Julie. I smiled again. Julie is the name my older sister and I used to call each other as a strange inside joke. I knew I would be okay.

Fairly soon I met my first psychiatrist ever. He was my age. He looked at me, saw my records and said, "I see women like you in here all the time. It's okay. We will get you started on a pediatric dose of meds, and make sure you do okay. The doctor you see when you leave here will probably raise the dosage."

"Women like me? What does that mean?"

"Women who are overwhelmed, anxious, have too much on their plate in life, and undealt-with traumas that all piled up and finally exploded."

"Oh."

I asked him how long I had to be there. It was a Thursday at this point. He said at least until Monday – five days, same as Angel had said. Monday was Halloween. I decided in my heart that I would go home Monday to be able to go trick-or-treating with my family.

I got settled into my room. As mentioned, they had taken all my belongings and gave them to Eric. Now I was told the rest of the rules: everyone had to wear loose-fitting clothes with no ties, straps, or strings. We were allowed one small pencil, like in mini golf. Any reading materials had to be cleared by the nursing staff.

We could have music on a stereo but no phones. The only phones allowed were those in the common area where everyone could hear us.

I lay on my small, hard bed and cried. Not long after, I received my first dose of medication and prayed that my system would tolerate it. It was a pediatric dose of another SSRI. They were hoping at such a small dose that I would not react. I was nervous to take another medication.

It was a strange feeling being settled and calm in a hospital. Others around me were on edge, one patient screaming out, one talking to many different people others could not see, and others detoxing from various drugs. I was uncomfortable, a little afraid, yet more at peace in my body than I'd been in weeks. I felt God's presence in my heart. I also recognized that I was only responsible for myself in the hospital.

On Friday morning, after breakfast and group therapy, I called Dad and Mom. I updated them as to why I was there, what was going on, and what I knew about the plan. Mom immediately planned to fly out the next day. (My parents moved back to Chicago in 2004.) My Dad was very concerned about me.

"Katie, how did this happen? How did you end up there with all the tools you know?"

"Dad, I must be doing research for my book. Every great author does her research." I said laughing and holding back tears, as I did not know the answer to his questions. I could only crack a very insensitive joke because I was still in a little bit of shock that I was there. I was being taught some big lessons about humility, grace, empathy, compassion, and love.

After I hung up with him, I went to sit on the patio. Grief stained my heart after hearing my dad's voice as we hung up the phone. I brought my journal, the only allowed book, with me out on the patio. It was the only outside area available to sit. It had bars like a jail cell blocking the concrete from the grass. All I could see were cement walls, some grass and bushes, and a small area of blue sky through the bars. So symbolic of what was happening in my inner world.

As I was journaling I kept asking God, "How did I get here? How did this happen? With all the tools that I know, really?!" I felt sad, angry, scared, and so confused. I was hunched over writing when I heard the patio doors open.

"Are you Kate?"

"Yes."

"I was told you want to see me."

"Who are you?"

"I am Pastor Preston."

"Of course you are."

I really did laugh out loud. I recall thinking, "That was fast, God. Thank you for listening." I sat in amazement.

I asked who sent him and he said one of the nurses. I did not ask to see a pastor, although I welcomed the visit.

We sat down together at one of those metal patio tables with the holes all across the top that you can drop things through. A paperclips was on the table, the shining silver reflecting off the thin stream of sunlight peeking through the metal bars. Strange, I thought. Paper clips were not allowed.

Pastor Preston began to talk with me about Jesus, as I shared my belief in Christ. I will never forget these words.

He said, "Kate. Even Christ had to come down from the mountain and be human to fulfill His purpose here. Even HE was not able to save Himself from the destruction of being human. When He left us His spirit, He left us the gifts needed to be able to be here in this world if we listened to Him. You have been trained in so many ways of healing and yet have not been trained in how to manage being human. It is time to process your experiences of human suffering and learn that your humanness is a gift too. It is God's way of having you do His work in this world. You will teach people Christ's teachings and ways to manage being human. You will help many."

I was floored. Totally speechless. Who was this man? I already knew who really sent him. We continued to talk for almost an hour. He shared many teachings with me and me with him. It was a Divine appointment. I felt as if I had been taken away to a private retreat, as no one came out on the patio the entire time we were talking. I wondered if it was all real. I had been given so many gifts of grace in just a few days, and was slowly beginning to understand and remember when Jesus said to me on my living room floor that I was never alone.

As the days went on I had to attend group therapy, and chose to work my way through the workbook they gave us on how to build emotional resilience. I figured if I was going to be there for four more days I needed to make the most of the time. I only had to focus on me, no one else. The workbook was helpful in guiding me to understand my codependency habits that I had yet to work through in therapy.

I learned how I had based my own sense of self-worth on my achievements, my education, my relationships, how other people felt about me, my success. I had no healthy sense of self in the truth of who I am, only in who I thought I needed to be in order to feel loved.

As I sat in these hour-long groups, some people talking, most listening, my heart softened.

What I discovered still brings tears to my eyes. There were about twenty of us on my side of the wing, ranging in age from seventeen to seventy-four. Everyone was there for different reasons, and yet in listening to each person's story I realized it was all the same and my heart was blown open in empathy for the common theme that at the end of the day we all want to feel safe and loved.

All of us, every single one, had a root story of "I am not good enough, and I am only lovable if..."

Whether there for drug detox or hallucinations, suicidal thoughts or attempts or severe panic, each person's story was built on the life of shame and not feeling loveable or loved.

I remember my yoga nidra teachings and my teacher talking about how "not good enough" was a root cause of so much suffering in this life. It becomes the bedrock that so many of us build the false story of our lives. Until we learn better.

It was then that I decided that perhaps PTSD could also stand for "Post-Traumatic Shame Disorder." A thought I still believe to this day, and after working with so many clients, holds true. It is the unprocessed shame that holds the heart hostage from receiving love, and the nervous system stuck in a trauma response. Shame is also the lowest emotional vibration. Perceived shame is what caused the separation in the Garden of Eden. Makes sense. The belief that we could ever be abandoned by God is absurd, yet it is the root cause of so much suffering.

By Saturday morning, I was doing well on the medication, not needing additional meds for breakthrough anxiety, and talking with other patients about yoga, mindfulness and meditation. I released a lot of judgment during my stay about why people would choose their suffering over their healing. I came to understand that it is often true that the pain we know, although uncomfortable and even causing great suffering, is safer to experience than the pain we don't know.

On the third day I was assigned a new nurse due to rotations. As I went to meet with him, I wondered if he would think I was crazy for my discussions on yoga and the like. He introduced himself.

His name was Michael and he wore a necklace with Jesus' face on it. I smiled, again thanking God for placing the perfect people on my path.

I was having a hard time accepting that I would have to be on meds. My ego and fear of pharmaceuticals were starting to get the best of me, and I felt resistant once again to taking them. Due to the past trauma of drugs, I knew that the fear was worse than the actual medication.

He said to me, "Kate. We are trying to get other patients here to learn a quarter of what you know about yoga, breathing, and meditation and help them get off some of the meds. You are resistant to taking one pill that could help you heal from this. If someone were to need insulin to help with diabetes would you tell them not to take it? Would you tell a heart patient not to take their heart meds because their heart doesn't function correctly without it?"

"No."

"Listen. Your nervous system and brain are not working right at this time. Let the medicine help you." He paused as if searching for a good example. "I'm a marathon runner. I have to take blood pressure regulating meds. I don't like to and yet I've tried other means and I need the meds."

"So what are you saying? I will need meds forever?"

"No. What I'm saying is, let the medicine help for now while you see if there are other ways to help yourself. There is no shame in taking meds except the shame you tell yourself."

Whew! That hit my heart like a dagger. There was that word again - shame – but this time reflected in a way that I had a choice to make.

He told me to set a goal. He said if someone wants to be a marathon runner they set their goal at 26.2 miles. Then they start working their way forward to get there by training the body and, even more so, the mind, to hit that goal. They don't start by running fifteen miles. They start with one.

I gave myself a goal to be off the meds within a year if I could. A part of me knew it may not be realistic, but I needed that goal.

And, though I did not know what that path looked like, I knew that as God was clearly with me, I would find my way.

I was called to check in with my doctor Saturday afternoon. He was happy with my progress. I asked if I could go home on Monday. He said he was off on Monday, but would write my release papers and the other psych doctor could approve if all went well Sunday, and I was not reacting to the medication.

I continued to attend group therapy and talk with other patients. I learned how important it is to be seen and heard in our healing journey. I learned that often a response is not needed to advise, yet a gentle, "I understand and I get it" could change someone's life path instantly.

I learned that we all yearn for connection, love, and belonging. I came to understand the deep ache inside the heart for compassion and understanding, and the way my body would armor up at the first mention of any judgment.

I learned that God is gracious and puts us in situations way outside our comfort zone to break us open a little more to the fragility of being human.

Sunday flew by and I was eagerly awaiting my appointment with the other doctor so I could be released. Admittedly, I was extremely nervous to go home because in the hospital I was only responsible for myself. At home I had two young kids, two dogs, a cat, a husband, and my own business, and all of that felt so overwhelming.

I opened the door to meet with the doctor who would decide if I was stable enough to go home. He was maybe ten years my senior and looked at me in a knowing way.

After introducing himself he asked me, "Where do you live?"

"Excuse me?"

"Where do you live? I would like you to be my patient when you leave here. I think I understand you."

I told him where I lived. Then I asked what he meant by "he understood me."

"I am a Ph.D. in Neuroscience, MD in psychiatry, a kundalini yoga teacher and Tai Chi Master. I have a feeling I know what you are going through and can help you understand."

Again, I laughed out loud. I was thinking, "Really, God? You are good, and this may be Your best yet."

He proceeded to tell me that he thought I was experiencing a Spiritual Awakening caused by all the years of training and accepting Christ in my life. My body was processing all the trauma out as it did not align with the new way of being. The new consciousness was bumping against the old consciousness and there was no space for both. My spiritual light was battling the darkness of trauma. This was the great battle within each of us. These were the triggers showing up in my system. My humanness was having a hard time integrating the changes. He promised he could help me and not have me on meds long-term. He reiterated again that he understood my journey.

I looked dazed. Did a medical doctor really just say those things?

He signed off on my release papers. I made an appointment with him for the following week.

I was going home the next day to be with my family on Halloween and take my kids trick-or-treating. I love Halloween and seeing them dressing up was one of my favorite joy moments.

I left on a Monday early afternoon. I had hit bottom, or maybe I was finally at the top seeing things clearly for the first time. The journey of reclaiming the pieces of me, and creating a life filled with joy moments had finally begun.

CHAPTER SIXTEEN

"THERE IS NOTHING WRONG WITH YOU."

After leaving the hospital, I found hope in knowing that my appointment with the well-reviewed endocrinologist referred by my general practitioner, was finally coming up. I was praying she would tell me I had some kind of auto-immune issue or something that would further explain the intense symptoms I was experiencing. I was not convinced that everything I was experiencing was due to trauma, and that perhaps a physical diagnosis of imbalance would mean a treatment plan.

My husband came with me on that first visit. When we entered the room my legs were once again shaking, a symptom I had come to accept as part of this anxiety that decided to join me each day.

I sat down on a chair, Eric next to me, awaiting the doctor to enter the room. When she did, she presented as strong, confident, yet comforting and approachable. After having been told by many friends not to expect much from an endocrinologist in terms of compassion or empathy, I was pleasantly surprised at her demeanor and bedside manner.

She sat down across from me, looked at me, and asked me to tell her what was going on. I went into a story about the past ten months: the various testing, medications, and reactions, leading up to my hospitalization a couple of weeks prior.

She asked if I was sensing any improvement with the medications. I told her I was not sure yet. My husband said, "A little bit." I had come to learn that often others notice changes faster than sometimes we do when we are in a constant trauma response.

I told her the story of feeling abandoned by my doctor. She shared that my doctor was basically saying that she did not know how else to help me, and referred me out to feel like she had done all she could. She agreed that stopping the hormones and psych meds cold turkey was not a good idea. She was also shocked at the amount of hormones in my system and said that this could definitely cause some mental/emotional imbalance. She said my blood readings did not make a case for hormone therapy.

She wanted me to have one more blood test done. And, since I was so concerned about diabetes, an irrational fear that developed during this time, she obliged my request for a blood sugar monitoring kit. I was to return in a couple of weeks to review the lab results, and those from monitoring my blood sugar each day.

During those two weeks, I had follow-ups with my psychiatrist, further testing by him, including a full panel of blood, genetic testing, and a test done to see my tolerance to well-prescribed medications on the market. Since I have a tendency to be sensitive to medication, he was concerned with prescribing without this information.

My psychiatrist helped me understand the true intent of psych meds, and provided continual support and assurance around how they could facilitate my healing journey. I was still very reluctant to use medication, yet felt trusting of his knowledge and deeper understanding of trauma and mental health.

My trust in him, and in the process, grew when the tests he ran showed that every medication I'd had an allergic reaction to was on my personal "do not use" list. Fascinating! Our blood and

DNA can show us what medications will work for our individual system and what we will react to adversely.

He also was able to show me that I was not presenting with any inflammatory symptoms, nor any genetic predispositions for specific diseases. I felt so blessed to have been given this holistic psychiatrist.

This doctor was also the one who taught me so much about what is called Post-Secondary Gain in any disease or imbalance. Post-Secondary gain is the benefit of staying stuck as the victim or as the one hurt or unwell, such as medical benefits, financial gain, emotional support, et cetera. To become well, therefore, means that those benefits or gains will go away.

I saw this often when working with clients with chronic pain. They would share their fear that if their pain went away their loved ones wouldn't come around as often, or they would lose their disability benefits and have to work again. As you can tell, this is a deep wound and support is essential to help these individuals get to the underlying reason for needing these gains.

My doctor asked me what the post-secondary gain was to my trauma, to the point that I was needing extra appointments with him. He questioned my marriage, my career, my happiness. I had to take a deep look at this.

What was revealed through my inner work with my trauma therapist was that my post-secondary gain was validation of my limiting belief that I was not good enough. Shame. Again, shame. If I recovered, this shame would be no longer and I wouldn't have any excuses for not living up to my potential. Shame had become my unconscious motivator, and the story I told myself was that if I didn't live in shame I may not feel loved. The two were entangled inside of me. Shame was the (unconscious) excuse for the trauma taking root in my system. Love was the unmet need.

When I returned to the endocrinologist a couple weeks later, she entered the room with a residential intern. She asked if I was okay with said intern staying in the room while we went over my results. While I wasn't okay with it, I said that I was, as I was still a really good people-pleaser at that time. Thankfully I am not that way anymore. My husband was next to me to my right, holding my hand. I was preparing for bad news.

She reviewed my blood labs and my blood sugar results. She looked at me as if I was the only one in the room.

"Kate, I am going to say something to you that I don't think anyone, and especially any doctor, has said to you. There is nothing wrong with you."

My eyes must have popped out of my head as my spine erected from its hunched posture. Tears started to form in my eyes.

All of these symptoms," she continued, "are due to the PTSD. Overall, yes your adrenals are fatigued. Yes, you are struggling with mental/emotional health. All of this is due to the unprocessed trauma. Keep doing your therapy and seeing your mental health providers. You will be okay. There is nothing wrong with you."

I started to cry, for two reasons:

1. I really wanted some kind of diagnosis that would help me know how to treat these terrifying symptoms.

2. There was nothing physically wrong with me. The mix of relief and confusion was a lot to hold in that moment.

Eric thanked the doctor. I asked if I needed to follow up with her. She said no.

When we left the office, and approached the car, I remember seeing a paperclip by my passenger door. I picked it up and placed it into my purse.

I left that day with further understanding of how trauma can create symptoms of disease, that while not medically diagnosable as illness, present exactly as if something is greatly wrong inside. This is often referred to as, "It's all in your head." For years I had low blood pressure, was checked for syncope (a loss of consciousness brought on by a dip in blood sugar), and had neurology appointments due to dizziness and brain fog. No one had ever asked about trauma or mental health.

A trauma-informed medical practitioner would say, "It's the trauma. You need trauma therapy." I came to learn that most medical professionals, including mental health therapists, are not trauma-informed. That requires additional training, and it is something you have to specifically request in your care.

While yoga tells us that there is nothing wrong with us, our ego wants to believe that if something is wrong, then the symptoms are justified and therefore possibly cured. If not curable, then at least they provide a rational understanding as to why you feel the way you do. The various holistic trainings I took were not trauma-informed, and in some ways exasperated the trauma symptoms.

If trauma-informed care was the norm in our society, emotional imbalances would be given the same amount, if not more attention, than the physical manifestations of those emotional imbalances.

I learned through this experience the importance of having all of my medical team, whether traditional or integrative, be trained in trauma-informed care. Since I have a sensitive nervous system, I needed providers who could meet me in that sensitivity and give me appropriate care to help remedy the reason for the imbalance. I didn't just want to manage my symptoms. I'd always believed in my ability to overcome them completely.

The belief that "nothing is wrong" with you refers to the deeper understanding that who you are as a being is not flawed. You are not what happened to you. Who you are is not defined by what you went through or by the residual symptoms you live with each day due to the unprocessed or processed experiences of your past.

I understand now that each symptom was my body's way of nudging me to release the pain I had been carrying around for so long. And, since I was so disconnected, the only way my body could get my attention was through intense emotional pain and uncomfortable body sensations to go with it.

What this endocrinologist did was give me another way to think of who I am. Prior to this, while I knew the teachings of yoga and Jesus tell us there is nothing wrong with us, I felt as if there was something deeply wrong with me.

Shame does that. It speaks and spews lies to make you live in fear and pain. It is also the way I survived the pain that often felt unsurvivable. The primary lie – that I was flawed – created a sense of security, until at some point the very thing that had protected me became the source of my suffering.

When I started learning Truth, the pain was no longer necessary. My internal battle, I realized, had stemmed from the conflict between my unprocessed trauma and the Wholeness of this Truth. It is, essentially, a struggle of the ego to survive. The problem is that it is often terrified of surrendering, when in fact surrender into Truth and Love is the very remedy needed to begin to soak the wounds in the healing balm of grace.

Once the egoic self knows the pain is over, and enough safety has been created in daily life, it can surrender that pain. Then you can honor it as an inner warrior of love, a part of you that took the wounds and protected you from the terror.

Now it is time for the ego to rest, for the inner child to feel loved, for the inner teenager to feel compassion and understanding, for all parts to feel protected by the greatest power of love that lives within us.

CHAPTER SEVENTEEN

IT TAKES A TEAM

A couple of weeks after seeing this endocrinologist, I saw the naturopathic doctor who specializes in homeopathic medicine. Homeopathy has been in my life since I was a teenager, a gift I'd been blessed with from Kent. I knew my body always responded well to this medicine, and I knew it did not cause conflict with any medication I was on from the psychiatrist. The psychiatrist was a huge supporter of this medicine and of Chinese Medicine. He also had me taking other supplements to support mineral and vitamin deficiencies.

The naturopath did a thorough case evaluation and said to me, "Kate, you are going to be okay. It will take time, and you will be okay." A voice of hope. A light in the darkness. She prescribed a certain homeopathic remedy that specifically matched each symptom of imbalance that I was having physically, mentally, emotionally, spiritually. I recall leaving that first appointment knowing that she was aligned with my heart, and was able to hold the space of hope that I really needed at that time.

I had received three messages of hope from three different medical practitioners – the psychiatrist, the endocrinologist, the naturopath. I also chose to continue to seek care from an additional practitioner, a well-reviewed Chinese Medicine doctor to support energetic imbalances, as I intuitively knew that my body needed additional care.

I went to see this Chinese Medicine doctor with an open heart and mind. He did a full intake, listened to parts of my story and why I was there with empathy and compassion. He checked pulses, read my tongue (a TCM technique for checking organ imbalances), and said he was going to use the PTSD protocol, called Taming the Dragon, to help balance my Qi, and bring harmony to my body, mind, heart, and spirit. He said my liver, spleen and kidney energies were out of balance, and I needed more blood. He said the nightmares were due to stagnancy in my energy and too much dampness (inflammation) in my body. He placed the needles all over me, five in the soft palate of my head, and a total of twenty-two at other various points in my body.

He invited me to "relax" as he turned on an infrared heat lamp over my belly. I laid there and breathed. A deep sense of peace and relaxation began to wash over me, one that I had not felt in a very long time. It reminded me of my experiences in yoga nidra when I was very aware of my body yet completely melted into bliss. I wanted to stay there forever, in that peacefulness and serenity that soothes the heart. I am pretty sure I fell asleep at some point, because when he walked in the room and said, "Okay," I woke up.

He took each needle out gently as I brought myself back fully.

He was standing at my left side, and placed a hand on my upper left arm. He patted my arm kindly and said, "You will be okay. Your heart just needs time to forgive. Keep praying to Jesus."

I started to cry. This man did not know my faith. He did not know that just a few weeks prior my husband and I chose to be baptized together at church after renewing our faith in Jesus as Lord and Savior. A sacred act of our love for each other and for Christ, and our renewed journey together.

The Chinese Medicine doctor did not know how I fell to my knees just four months prior, screaming at Jesus to help me. He did not know the depth of the pain I was experiencing over the harm that had been caused to my soul. He did not know that it was due to my faith that I was even in his office, able to function and show up each day. He did not know how Divinely orchestrated each day had been since I chose to live and begin the faith walk.

Something in him knew all of this and more. He, too, gave me the gift of hope that day. God uses people. This I know as Truth. All of these practitioners, in addition to the unconditional love from my family, became foundational support as I slowly began to rebuild my life on the anchor of faith, hope, and love.

CHAPTER EIGHTEEN

GOD IS MY PAPERCLIP

Over the course of many weeks of doctors' appointments and time off work for my well-being, I found paperclips everywhere and in the strangest of places. The first was the one I mentioned at the hospital, on the patio table. Sometimes they would be on the ground, one was in the refrigerator, and one in my clothes dryer. I came to realize that there must be some greater meaning in all of this. Spirit will go to all lengths to get attention when you need to receive a message. Why all the paperclips? Such an odd sign.

As I mentioned earlier, our church was enormous, with hundreds of seats. One Saturday evening Eric and I headed there early to find seats a little closer to the front. As we walked into an aisle to sit down, there, on my seat was one single paperclip. I looked all around at the other seats. No other paperclips.

I sat down for worship, laughing a bit inside. Eric laughed, too. What is with all the paperclips, God?

I immediately heard this response: "I am your paperclip. I hold everything together for you. You do not have to do this on your own. Trust Me to guide you and take care of you. Surrender in faith to My love and know I am always with you. You are never alone and always loved. I've got this. You can rest."

Some people find pennies, or heart-shaped rocks. Others see feathers, and listen for certain sounds or even smells. For whatever reason, the reminders of faith came to me in the form of a paperclip.

Paperclips continued to mark my path weekly. I recall one day struggling with shameful thoughts. I was going into the grocery store to grab a few things. I asked God to give me a paperclip to let me know I was cared for and supported.

I searched and searched for a paperclip. When I left the store, I headed to my therapy session. When I walked into the office, my therapist handed me a box. She said, "I saw this and had to get it for you. May it remind you."

Inside the box was a silver paperclip necklace. Of course, I cried.

Paula, my therapist, moved out of the country in March of 2017, the same month my psychiatrist informed me that he was no longer going to see patients in private practice. He was focusing on in-patient treatment centers only. One year from the time I'd started to decline, I was being faced with the opportunity to practice gratitude for these amazing practitioners and their care, and support my life during a time of crisis. This also helped me strategically process my abandonment wounds.

Paula referred me to Darla, another trauma therapist in her office. Darla, who was working on her doctorate, was also a trained yoga teacher and a shaman. Another God-wink on my healing path. My psychiatrist referred me to a partner in the practice. She was kind, understanding, and aware of my goal to come off all psych meds within a year.

Darla asked if she could use me as her case study for her doctoral thesis on somatic therapies for PTSD. I said yes. Her book knowledge combined with my background as a yoga therapist and my soul knowledge from God, turned into a powerful experience of inner discovery and healing.

While this time of transition was very difficult, I held onto the promises God gave me for deliverance and grace. In a time of prayer, God said to me, "Kate, write a list of all the ways I have delivered you already. Once that list is done, you will realize that I am worthy of your trust. I will deliver you from this pain, and I will use all of it for good. I promise."

I made the list as guided. Pages of remembrance of so many moments of mercy and grace. So many paperclips moments.

When I started working with Darla she told me that soon I would be experiencing a wide range of emotions that would be very uncomfortable to feel: anger, sadness, resentments, bitterness, rage, grief, and more. She said that the rage was coming soon and to prepare myself for this experience. She shared that it would feel very primal and animalistic. It would be as if I wanted to crawl on the ground, growl, roar, scream, and fight. Darla assured me that this is a common part of the trauma recovery journey, and said it was important to be prepared so when it came I would know how to take care of myself. She had me download certain music to help myself process it out, music with drumbeats and certain gongs, and vibrational sounds. It was a very shamanic approach and I was grateful for the connection.

Well, she was right. Not long after her verbal set-up, I was home alone doing my yoga practice when suddenly I felt a huge burst of rage. I screamed violently out loud. I am surprised that my neighbors didn't come check on me. I took out a notebook and found a pen. I stabbed, scribbled, raged in what looked like child's handwriting and indescribable drawings. I rolled on the floor, growling, howling, punching pillows and yelling. As fast as it started, it stopped. When it stopped, everything became silent. The kind of silence where you can hear that faint whisper of electronic buzzing. I sat down, closed my eyes, and dropped into a deep state of peace.

This rage would continue to move through me for a few months, each time needing its space to be held, loved, expressed and nurtured. It was a very young part of me that didn't have a voice or words to use to share the pain inside. Sometimes it felt very scary, as it occurred when I was driving alone one afternoon. I quickly pulled into a parking lot, turned on loud music, and screamed "FUCK!" many times in a row and as loud as I could. I was parked very far back. When I came out of the energy, there was a paperclip sitting on the dashboard of my car, right in my line of sight.

I knew at that moment that I was being carried through this experience of intense emotional pain as I took steps closer to freeing myself from the chains of my past.

I don't know what you believe in. I don't know how you connect to any, if any, higher power of choice. I do know that when one is willing, there are signs and messages everywhere. Still, to this day, I find paperclips all the time. Whenever I find one, I notice what I am thinking about, and I surrender it to God, knowing He is holding it all together. I can rest.

I receive emails and social media messages from students and clients all the time showing me the places they find paperclips and are instantly reminded of faith and God's grace.

Search for your paperclip. Let it bring you peace in times of questioning your connection to Love. Sometimes these simple reminders of hope can change your entire day.

CHAPTER NINETEEN

FORGIVENESS

In July of 2017, while visiting family in Chicago, I heard God say to me, "It's time to begin to forgive." I was not sure I was ready to forgive, nor was I sure I wanted to. A part of me still believed my abusers didn't deserve forgiveness. Honestly, I'm pretty sure a part of me said, "Fuck that!"

What I did feel was this deep aching inside to be freed from the anger and resentments that I harbored towards people from my past who had hurt me in ways I pray no one has to experience yet unfortunately are all too common in this world.

I knew what I needed to do, maybe not what I wanted to do. I decided it would happen when I went to the beach one afternoon. I knew by now not to argue with God. I shared with Eric what I was going to do. While he didn't think it was necessary, as he was still processing the anger within him at what happened to me, he knew that once I set my heart on something it was going to happen.

My family and I went to Evanston Beach outside of Chicago. I began to walk down the shores of Lake Michigan as I often would as a child. I was asking God for a sign so I would know it was time.

Blue glass rocks were always special to my family, and if you found one, I believed it was a message from God. I walked that beach from one end to the other, and as I came to the very end where I could go no further, I found one blue glass rock, one white feather, a clear glass rock, and a light teal blue glass rock.

I went up to my husband and said it was time.

We walked along Lake Shore Drive to the cemetery across from the lake. Not a bad place to be laid to rest, I must say.

We traveled up the paved drive seeking the gravestones of my grandparents, who had been buried there in 1999. That was the last time I had been to this cemetery, seven months before the overdose.

We walked up and down trying to find their markers. I remember I called Dad, and he was trying to help guide me to where it was. As we were about to give up, I turned around and found myself right over their graves.

A feeling of deep pain, sorrow, and grief flooded my body as I got on my knees before their graves.

This man. This monster. How dare he do the things to me and others that he did. How dare she know and never stop any of it. I was fuming. Anger steamed inside of me as I felt this desire to rage at their graves and demolish their stones. I recall letting the feelings move through me, my husband holding space for me to emote and process.

He said, "You know you don't have to do this. It's okay not to be ready to forgive him. You don't ever have to forgive him."

I started crying. Tears pouring down my cheeks. My body was shaking and shuddering as my nervous system started to release the emotion locked inside for thirty years.

I was gripping the glass rocks and feather in my hands, rocking back and forth over their decomposed bodies beneath the earth. As fast as the intensity of rage and tears came on, they softened and a peace moved through me.

The winds calmed down and I heard, "It's time, Kate. You deserve to be free. In starting the process of forgiving them, you are giving yourself permission to be free."

I looked down at their names engraved in the stones, covered by overgrown grass and weeds. I took the light teal rock and placed it on my grandmother's grave, telling her, "I am willing to forgive you. I forgive you so I am free and so your soul can heal."

Then, with shaking hands, I took the blue glass rock, the white feather, and the clear glass rock. Calling on the power of the Holy Spirit, I placed them on my grandfather's grave and said, "I am willing to forgive you. I forgive you so I can be free and so your soul can heal."

I bent forward and sobbed, hands clenched in the earth as my body began a healing shift deep inside.

It was done. I heard the voice of one of my past healers say, "You did good. It is done. Go now. This will take some time but know the deepest healing has now begun."

Eric took my hands, surrounding me in his warm embrace, telling me how brave and strong I am, and gently guiding me back towards the magical sounds of the lake waves crashing into the rocks along the shore.

As we walked along the drive, I saw a Purple Heart cemented into the concrete. I understood. Purple is the vibration of bravery, courage, sacrifice, and the color of forgiveness. This was a validation of the work done.

We left the gates of the cemetery behind and crossed the road to see the water and its majesty of power washing away the old and receiving the new. I laughed and giggled with joy. A strange lightness of energy bouncing through my body that I had not felt in years.

I climbed the rocks by the shoreline, and took Warrior pose, the wind blowing my hair back in the breeze and my heart valiantly open with a new surge of reclaimed joy spiraling through my body.

As we walked back to the beach to join my family, I found a single paperclip in the sand. I picked it up and smiled. A paperclip on the beach. Thanks, God.

It is a day I will remember forever. The beginning of a new life birthed by the fires of forgiveness. A day when I reclaimed my power from my past by no longer allowing it to hold me hostage in anger and resentment. It was only the beginning, as I knew that to choose to forgive begins an unwinding of the spiral of energy built upon the pain from the past.

You can't fake forgiveness. You must be ready. I was ready to move forward. Forgiveness is not a one-and-done experience. It is a daily commitment to choosing to love yourself, even when the pain of the past is trying so hard to overcome you again. I continued in weekly therapy with Darla, using EMDR with a body-centered approach. Each week I would journey into a part of my body to reclaim a part of me left behind in many moments of pain. Jesus and Mother Mary would always join me on these journeys, as their energetic presence would help me find the strength to keep going when I felt stuck. Darla would facilitate a loving space, while I self-led the inner journey. Her words were a grounding anchor into present-moment reality, while I traveled between dimensions to bring harmony to my soul.

January 2018, fifteen months after the hospital, six months after that day in the cemetery, hundreds of hours in weekly therapy sessions, endless hours of my own therapeutic practices, I walked into my therapist's office, finally ready to do another big piece on forgiveness.

She had me lay down on her couch, holding the EMDR buzzy pads in my hands. There would be no light tracking today. She asked me to check in with my body, to notice where I was holding the tension. It was my upper back, always my upper back when it came to forgiveness.

I closed my eyes. She turned on the pads. It didn't take me long to journey into my body. I saw myself back in the golden temple with the emeralds, rubies, sapphires, amethysts all over the walls. The altar was in the corner with the four books, however, this time there were only three books on it. The large mahogany oval table with twelve chairs around it.

I saw a doorway back to the left that gave entrance to a larger library of books and long hallways. All the chairs at the table were taken and one was open at the head of the table closest to where I walked into the temple. This place really is magnificent.

As I approached the table and saw the people sitting, I was in a little bit of shock. There to the right of me was my grandfather, my grandmother, the guy who'd raped me on prom night, the guy involved in the overdose situation, and two others involved that night. They were all seated to my right. On my left were Mother Mary, Jesus, Kent, Connie (another very special shaman healer of mine), Archangel Michael, and God. God appeared as a male energy, my mind creating him to look like Gandolf from Lord of the Rings. They were all to my left around the table.

I sat down at the head of the table. Back to my far right I saw myself at seventeen, scared and shaking. My six-year-old self was standing on my left side by the arm of the chair, next to Mother Mary.

I saw books sitting open in front of each person to my right. I saw a book open in front of me. There were two large stamps placed next to each other just beyond my book. One was red and one was green.

I looked over at seventeen-year-old me and asked her to come to me. She reluctantly walked over and stood at my right side. I looked up at her and smiled.

Three of me at once. Me at six years old, me at seventeen years old, me at thirty-seven years old, all there together for this experience.

My therapist would occasionally stop the alternating buzzing tappers in my hands to have me check in with my body. I was very aware of laying on her couch, with her watching, sensations in my physical body, and this spiritual journey happening within me all the while.

I looked all around the table, wondering what was to happen. My grandfather wouldn't hold my gaze. My grandmother looked very sad and hunched over slightly. The ex who raped me was ignorant and did not understand why he was there. My other ex was adamant that he'd done nothing wrong, that he was the one who tried to help me, and the others involved that night were almost faceless.

God spoke to me, saying, "Kate, you have a decision to make. What was done to you was wrong on all accounts. You get to make this decision for yourself now. It is time. This decision also affects you. You must decide whether you will forgive these people for what they did to you, or whether you will condemn them for their acts of harm. You will use the stamps, red to condemn, green to forgive, and stamp their books. It is time to decide."

I remember in my body it felt very intense and heavy on my heart. My legs felt a little antsy and tingly. I recall my therapist stopping at this point to check in with me and see if I felt ready for this.

I told her, "It is happening and I know what I need to do."

I was quickly back at the table, holding the hands of six-year-old me and seventeen-year-old me. I looked at them both, knowing this decision was the right one for me.

My guides were silent, holding space for this massive process taking place in my subconscious mind and multidimensional state.

I let go of the hands of my younger selves. I took the stamp in my right hand, my left hand bracing myself over the table as I leaned over, the books each being pushed in front of me. I stamped each book with a thump, "Forgiven" in bright emerald-green letters across the open page on each book. Six books stamped with Forgiveness.

I sat back down and God reached over and took a blue stamp from his hands and placed it down on my book.

"Kate, because you have chosen to forgive, you are FREE."

The word "FREE" marked in royal blue on the pages of my book.

My six-year-old self immediately jumped into my body. My seventeen-year-old self lifted her head and shared a faint sigh of relief. She chose to merge into my heart. Each person on the right side of the table got up and was taken out of the temple. I never said a word to any of them.

It was finished. Love had won.

I came out of EMDR in tears, relief-stricken through my whole body. A new kind of lightness and weightlessness that was different than any other felt before. My therapist smiled and said, "Amazing. Thank you for letting me witness this sacred act."

I left her office that day different. The forgiveness journey would continue, and still does, as there are days when I must choose to forgive when I find myself frustrated by the ways my nervous system still reacts, even though life is very beautiful now. It is a continual choice that gets easier with time.

I believe to forgive is the most courageous inner work we can do. Forgiveness of others and forgiveness of ourselves. It frees us from being a hostage to our past pain. It creates an opening for new life. It is the balm to old wounds that had a scab reopened too many times.

While forgiveness does not make what happened okay, nor does it make you forget what happened, it does allow for you to move forward without the hate, bitterness, and resentment in your heart. I wanted to be free, which meant I chose to make forgiveness a daily part of building a new life based on compassion and love.

LEARNING HOW TO LET GO

I remember one morning in spring 2006, talking to Kent while driving on the freeway on my way to work. I was in retail management at the time, and four months pregnant with my son. I was complaining to Kent about where I lived, how much I disliked the desert and wanted to move. How I'd never chosen to be there, how I was made to move at seventeen. Though Kent knew the story, he listened intently.

At the end of my ranting he said to me, "Kate, you need to learn what you can control and what you can't. Do you have any control over what happened to you at seventeen at this point in time? Do you have control over the decision your parents made at that time?"

"No, to both."

"Something I learned a long time ago. I ask myself this question: 'Do I have control over this?' If the answer is no, then I choose to let it go. If the answer is yes, then I ask myself, 'What do I want to do about it?', shifting my energy to taking control of what I can and letting go of the rest.' He continued, "Kate. Geography doesn't matter. Where you live is not the problem here. There is something deeper that needs your attention, and when you are ready it will reveal itself."

I'm pretty sure I was just pissed off at him at that point, and I knew he was aware of that. It used to make me so frustrated when he went into these vague spiritual teachings, yet not explain to me what he knew that I did not know, well aware that he knew I did not know yet.

More times than I care to count, when I would bring up things from the past, I would be met with: "You need to let that go already. Haven't you done enough work on that already? Why are you still so caught up in that story? Why are you allowing your past to hold you hostage like that? Just let it go already. Let it go."

I kept questioning myself and wondering why I was so hung up on the past. Why was I so angry all the time? Why did I want to run from a life that was pretty amazing?

In my first two-hundred-hour yoga teacher training program, I began to understand the idea of attachment, unhealthy attachment and healthy attachment. Unhealthy attachment causes suffering. Healthy attachment creates safety. The teachings of yoga explain that at no time do we want to be attached to anything that can change our identity or concept of who we are. In developmental psychology, healthy attachment allows for a child to thrive, and develop into healthy autonomy as an adult. Unhealthy attachment, known as attachment disorders, creates unmet needs, internal instability, developmental trauma, and often mental illness.

The yoga teachings go on to teach that who I am is love. It is the unchanging essence of creation itself. This mirrors the biblical teachings that say we are children of God, perfectly made in His image, which is love. We have never been separated from this love.

When I find my identity in this love, I am always safe. Any suffering that comes in life is then based on identifying myself as something fleeting, like a cloud in the sky. I began to understand this concept of letting go. I needed to learn how to let go of all the ways I have identified who I am by anything other than God's love for me, and as the being of love that I am.

This seemed daunting and exhausting. After a therapy session, I created a list of all my self-labeled identities. Wife. Mother. Daughter. Friend. Sister. Marketer. Yoga Teacher. Housekeeper. Makeup Artist. Daughter-in-Law. I wrote out all the roles I played in life and began to realize how I created a story about myself based on each of these roles.

In each role, I was always not good enough. I was always comparing, even when I was great at what I did. I was always trying to prove. I was always causing so much suffering for myself seeking external love because at that time I did not believe God loved me, and I certainly did not believe I was worthy of love. I absolutely did not believe that I was good enough or enough in general.

In fact, I remember writing in my journal about my hatred for the word "enough." I did not want to be enough. It felt limiting. It felt like settling. It felt like, "Who wants to be good enough? I want to be great." I was in so much avoidance of what I now know to be living in the veils of shame that I could not see where I was the one causing so much pain in my life.

I remember my teacher saying to me in yoga nidra training, "Events happen in life and we may get hurt – physically or emotionally. It happened once, maybe more than once. After the event is over, we have a choice. We can let the door close and move forward, or we can keep slamming that same door in our own face, constantly reminding ourselves of the pain. So often we choose to keep slamming that door in our own face."

Why is that? Shame. The feeling of being unworthy, unlovable, unwanted. These root wounds that we take on at such a young age that we may not even remember a life without them. They infiltrate our entire nervous system and cause us to believe lies about who we are. Believing these lies actually kept me safe; the lies helped me to survive what was trying to kill me inside.

It is not the event itself that causes the trauma. The trauma is the unprocessed emotions stuck in the nervous system, activated by anything similar in energy that happens throughout your day.

This happened. I must not be good enough. I must have deserved that. It must have been my fault. No one will understand. I can't tell anyone. He threatened me so I must not be safe. I need to change who I am to belong here. They don't care. Maybe I don't belong here. If I belonged here, why would this be happening to me? If I was wanted, why is life so painful? I must be broken. I must be damaged goods now.

All lies. Every single one of them. Complete and utter lies that I believed to be true out of a false sense of safety for survival.

These beliefs and the identities formed around them are a really confusing way that our being creates safety and survival. In actuality, it is a brilliant part of us that steps in to say, "Believing this to be true may keep you safe right now, so while it is not true, I need to believe it to be true to make it out of this situation, and have my needs met, because I cannot meet my own needs at this time."

Sure. As a child, we are not saying this. I just imagine this is the agreement that I made with myself at that time in my life where I was terrified and somewhere in my psyche I knew what I needed to do to protect myself, to keep myself safe, and to get my emotional needs met.

I became the perfect little chameleon, and stayed that way until I was thirty years old. I had no idea who I was nor what I wanted. I had ideas of what I thought I wanted, and I had ideas of what I thought I was supposed to want in life. I also had ideas that no one knew anything about because to share them would be breaking norms, changing patterns, and beginning to be me, not who I thought the world, society, family and friends wanted me to be.

Yoga teaches you how to bring all the ways you don't love yourself into the light so you can embrace your wholeness and remember that you are whole. You are love. Just as you are right now! Learning how to let go began with my yoga journey; a journey of learning to love who I am, not who I pretended to be.

Jesus teaches us that we are made in the image of God. We are already whole. We need to remember who we are in Him, not who we are perceived to be in this world.

We need to understand that to let go means to surrender to safety in love. As I continued in my training, I began to understand that in order for me to learn how to let go, I needed to learn what I really have control over in my life, just as Kent said to me in that conversation on the phone.

It was a brutal awareness when I put pieces together and came to the understanding that I really only have control over four things:

1. My breath
2. My thoughts
3. My emotions
4. My actions

That's it. That is all that I have control over. That is all you have control over. Nothing more. Nothing less. That may seem relieving or terrifying. How often are you trying to control what you have no control over? I can honestly say that I used to spend the majority of my time trying to manage and control that which I have absolutely no control over – the external world.

Yoga taught me to take control of my breath. The breath is the manager of the mind and energy. When the breath is calm, the mind is calm and eventually clear. When the mind is clear, the thoughts are steady. When thoughts are steady, emotions are regulated. When emotions are regulated, actions are rational and reasonable.

This simple, yet profound skill of taking conscious control over my breath created so much space for awareness of where I was causing my own suffering. It helped me learn that I am not my thoughts nor my emotions. I am the witness and observer of my thoughts and emotions. I can notice them and let them pass. I can control them, and I can choose them.

It is only when one becomes witness to their thoughts that they learn to control their mind. In order to control their mind, they must be aware that they are not the thought, they are the one noticing the thought.

This idea may seem confusing, and the best way I have ever heard it described is a quote from a Buddhist teacher, Pema Chodron.

"You are the sky. Everything else – it's just the weather."

We all know that storms come, and storms go. Some storms stay longer, some pass through rather quickly. If we only see the storm, we forget the blue sky and the sun. If we identify as the storm, we have forgotten we are the sky, not the storm. This is the cause of the suffering.

If our emotions are the byproducts of our thoughts, then by learning to control our thoughts, we can then learn to control our emotions. It can get a little sticky when we feel like our emotions happen faster than our thoughts can process them.

This is where we have to practice conscious breathing. We need to create space between the thoughts and the emotions. Most of the time we are not aware of what we are thinking, and therefore only become aware of what we are feeling due to the experiences in our body.

If our actions in life are based on reactions, meaning re-acting to the situation as if it has happened before, then we need to learn how to be present in the moment and respond, not live life re-acting to the past.

The breath is the key to presence. You cannot breathe yesterday's breath nor your breath from ten years ago. You cannot breathe a breath ten minutes from now nor ten years from now.

Each breath, every inhale and every exhale is happening at this moment.

As you become aware of your breath, then the controller of your breath, you will naturally become aware of your thoughts, and the controller of your thoughts.

When your thoughts are clear, your emotions will become more manageable and not hijack your nervous system, causing a reaction. Instead your breath will manage your thoughts, giving space for your emotions to pass by, so you can then take reasonable action.

You may be wondering, "What does this have anything to do with learning how to let go?"

When we begin to understand that we are the sky not the weather, we can begin to see the weather for what it is, weather. The storm is not who we are. The anxiety is not who we are. The story of the past is not who we are. The identities that we self-label as our pains are not who we are.

We have the capacity to hold all of it, yet attach to none of it. I don't imagine that the sky says to the cloud, "Hey, stay a little longer, would ya? Could you make it thunder more? How about a tornado right now?"

No. The sky does not say that. The sky has no preference for what is passing through. It is just holding a space for it to pass through. Sunshine. Storms. All of it. The sky is neutral, yet allowing for it all.

As we learn to identify as the sky, as love, as the capacity to hold all the experiences of being human, we begin to let go of our identity to anything that can change. We begin to understand that everything is impermanent except for the love of God, and every part of our being is held by the love of God.

The foundation upon which you build your life shifts from a false sense of safety built upon trauma into a foundation of faith built upon love.

If I know who I am in the image of God, then the energy of love that is alive within me becomes my guiding light. I call it Holy Spirit. Yoga calls it remembering you are whole-in-spirit, and you are then able to see all of life from a place of wholeness instead of woundedness.

Learning how to let go means beginning to remember who you are, and to clear out all the clouds in your sky that you have attached to as who you are, to remember you have always been and will always be whole. You have been and will always be enough. You have been and will always be loved.

We can understand that to let go is to give ourselves the freedom to finally be held in love, not controlled by fear. We begin to understand that fear is a part of us from the past, stuck in the storm, unsure of how to move forward. When fear is held by love, it integrates.

I came to understand that love is the greatest power we could ever hold, and to try and manage love is to play God, and that is not my job. My job is to accept all of me and love all of me.

I realized that when someone was saying, "Let it go," what they were really saying was, "Let love in and let it hold all of you – your pain, your past, your present, your anxiety, your fear, your joy, your sorrow, your peace."

This is not an easy process and will ask more of you than you imagine. It will ask that you look in the mirror and say to yourself, "I love myself. I am good enough. I am great enough. I am loved. I am lovable. I am wanted. I am valuable. I am capable. I belong here. I have a right to be here. I am purposeful."

Love will ask you to clear out all the lies, to clear the pathways of pain that have been intruding on your heart and mind. Love will ask that you go into the dark to embrace all the parts abandoned and exiled in pain, and bring them into the light to be nurtured and held.

Your body will shake. Your nervous system will unwind. This is why safety is priority number one.

Love will say to you, "I will love you until you remember that you are love."

Love will fight for you. Love will hold you. Love will be the rock that you anchor into as the grounding of new life.

Love will ask that you surrender all the suffering and trust that you will be given something far more amazing in return.

Love will ask that you set boundaries and if you don't know how, you will learn how.

Love will ask that you no longer abandon yourself, and instead learn how to hold each part of you with the tenderness and gentleness that you would a newborn baby.

Love will ask you to look fear in the eye and say, "Yes, I love you too," as fear is simply a part of you that has been seeking your own love for a very long time.

I have learned that to let go is to let love lead. When I lean into love and soften into the safety of that holding, I am free.

Love is the ultimate Truth.

CHAPTER TWENTY-ONE

BEFRIENDING THE BODY

Since I was in junior high, exercise was an outlet for stress and body shame. I used exercise as a way to feel better about myself, and to avoid feeling anything at all.

As I shared earlier, I decided to play basketball and volleyball through middle school and my freshman year of high school. I was fairly good at both, and enjoyed being on a team. I realized that by practicing, running, and playing in games, I was getting stronger, leaner, more encouragement, and more praise. My heart was yearning inside for these things, and I started to find them in sports.

I played the game in my head, using my body. I think that is how most people live their lives. I had no body awareness, and I didn't know that.

My mind wasn't exactly a healthy place to be. I was constantly in my thoughts, though not aware of them at all, and I was simply trying to make it through junior high. Middle school girls are not kind. I'm sure you know that.

Exercise became an excuse to avoid how I felt and to numb out the pain in my heart. Every time I felt a pull, I would exercise. This continued in high school, until I tore my left ACL playing basketball freshman year.

Dribbling the ball down the right lane, going in for a lay-up against an opponent, I came down hard on my left foot and felt a pop. Down I went on the court, not getting back up. Refs came over. Coaches come over. Friends come over. I was in a daze.

I tried to get up and couldn't put weight on my foot without my knee giving out. I knew something was wrong. They asked if I could shoot the free throw because I guess I was fouled on the play. I don't remember.

I couldn't stand up on my own to do it. I went to sit on the bench. This would be the last school basketball game for me.

A day or two later I went for an MRI. A partial tear, no surgery needed. Physical therapy was ordered by my orthopedic, then re-evaluate. One day in physical therapy they had me doing a lateral lunge, and snap. Yep, now a partially torn ACL became a full torn ACL.

Surgery happened within a week. I remember going to the hospital, the IV, starting to count backward, and then waking up with the breathing tube still in my mouth. I had a hard time coming out of anesthesia. I reacted to the pain meds with fevers, earaches, and vomiting. No pain meds for me beyond ibuprofen.

In 1996, ACL recovery was six months, with little mobility for the first few. I started with a new physical therapist that treated the whole being, and three times weekly treatments with Kent.

I recovered much faster than the usual patient. My orthopedic was not surprised as he'd worked with Kent for other patients too. My physical therapist was intrigued about my fast progress, and I was curious about his integrative approach.

It was at that time that I slowly started to understand the kinesiology of the body, the relationship to the mind, and the functional understanding of how the movement of the knee is based upon the strength and flexibility of the feet, core, and hips. Before he would do things to strengthen my knee, I had to do the things to strengthen all that surrounded my knee.

I was amazed, and at fifteen years of age decided I wanted to be a physical therapist who did energy work, and help people the way he and Kent helped me. This experience helped me begin to understand and feel my body, to study the body/mind complex in other ways. Interesting how pain does that.

I would continue to see Kent to have him help me physically, while being so curious about the energy work he did to balance out what he called the physical, etheric, and auric bodies. These are terms that I would not understand for many years, yet it made so much sense at the same time.

I quickly became more enchanted with the energy bodies than my physical body, and used this knowledge to continue to dissociate or disconnect from the discomforts of my past and emotions, using the excuse that I could avoid it in the energy realm.

This process is called spiritual bypassing; that is, using spiritual gifts and understanding to bypass the suffering of being human. The problem with this gift is that at some point, if you are fortunate, something will happen in life that causes you to have to feel your body and repair the pain causing you to want to leave it.

Dissociation is a term used to describe the capacity to disconnect from your present moment experience, and either disappear into a daydream or possibly regress to reliving an experience of the past. Most often this was a developed skill due to traumatic experiences where one needed to leave the feeling body to survive the event and, depending on the frequency of the event happening, became a survival skill. It is an extreme parasympathetic response of the nervous system, and a necessary one if survival is threatened.

Please know that this is an unconscious action of the nervous system and brain to work together to keep you safe. The problem with this reaction is that it can happen without you knowing, at times when there is no imminent danger. This can cause you to miss out on a lot of life and block out a lot of joy because you are not experiencing life, you are simply going through the motions.

Life is meant to be experienced through the senses. When there is a program of dissociation developed for survival, it can become addicting, just like anything else. It can become a way to avoid life, instead of being present to it. Once I learned how it felt to be out-of-body, I could do it at will. A great way to only enhance my desire to not feel my body and the emotional suffering waiting for me inside.

The injury to my ACL was my first call back to my body, yet I was not ready to listen. After going through full recovery, I was back to regular exercise, and chose to focus on volleyball training, my other sport of choice, instead of going back to basketball.

Weightlifting, running, drills – all to try and improve before the next season. Long story short, I didn't make the team my junior year, and I still remember leaving the gym feeling defeated and torn inside. As the coach said, "Yes, you put in a ton of effort, and you still are not good enough. Missing a season cost you, and you didn't make the team."

I immediately blamed my body – how dare it have an ACL injury that caused me to miss sophomore year of volleyball, thus causing me to not make the team, even with my best efforts and hard training.

My late teens and half of my twenties were spent using my body to try to be how I wanted it to be. It wasn't until I was twenty-six and took my first yoga class that I understood the nature of my body. As I shared earlier in the book, my husband purchased me a gift certificate telling me I needed to de-stress and get a hobby. I was not taking good care of myself after having my son, and while I preferred running and weightlifting, I figured I would give yoga a try. How hard could it really be?

I got my ego handed to me in that first class, and by the time we laid down in savasana I was sweaty and exhausted. I also felt deeply relaxed. I was not sure what happened until after savasana, when I had this thought: "There is something very different about this yoga stuff."

I went back the next day, and the day after that. Yoga became my muse, and my way of understanding how to integrate all the things I understood about energy, with the physical body. It was the start of a new way of life that I definitely didn't see coming.

The instructor during each class would call out many alignment cues for each pose, and even come by to physically adjust my body in the pose if I was not in the right alignment. While at this time I greatly appreciated the correction, I learned over time that this particular style of yoga, which I practiced for over five years, was just reaffirming my "not good enough" story and deepening my trauma-response about perfection.

Every time I went into a pose I hoped for praise from my teacher and would realign to perfect the pose. It was not until my advanced yoga teacher training program and yoga therapy program that I understood yoga postures were not a place for perfection; that was not the intent.

The poses in yoga are to create space for more prana, or life force, to move through you. Your breath is the vehicle that moves prana through the body. Therefore, when you combine intentional movement with conscious breathing, the more life force you have moving through your being. If God is the source of life, and He breathed life (prana) into us, then as more prana is moving through the deeper our connection with God. As we become more deeply connected with God, we remember the Truth of who we are, Love.

Where we get stuck in a pose, and send the breath to that area in the body, this life-giving energy, over time, dissolves the stuck energy. The darkness is brought to the light. Love has won again.

The body-based practice is one small part of the path, and it happens to be the one that most westerners start as their yoga.

The other seven limbs on the eight-limb path are more important than the poses, however, if one does not have the awareness of the physical body, the other seven limbs can be more difficult to embody.

In any trauma-based recovery program, an integral piece is building a new relationship with the body as a place of safety and sense of security, instead of a place of constant suffering. This piece can take many years to reprogram, as the physical body was the holder of the memories of the trauma. Each time the body is activated, there is potential for the memory to reappear, and if it is not held in the safe container of compassion, connection, and belonging, that memory could cause a trauma response, deepening the already ingrained pattern of trauma.

In my own therapy sessions, by using the body I began to overcome the need to disconnect from my body in times of stress. My yoga practice helped me find presence, control, and empowerment over the sensations in my body. I could choose how intense the sensations were in each pose, and if I wanted to stay in the pose or choose to come out. I used yoga poses and breathwork to help me learn how to regulate my nervous system.

This is offered in the physical practice of yoga by using the poses to teach you how to feel your body again in a safe way. Each pose intentionally creates stress on the muscles of the body, thus causing a sensation inside. These sensations are neutral, until the mind begins to associate the sensation with an experience from the past that may or may not have been emotionally charged, and incomplete. Just as the earlier water and bathtub metaphor, you need to feel enough sensation to notice it, yet not too much to overcome you.

If the experience of these sensations was one of trauma, whether conscious or unconscious, the person in the pose now has a choice to either stay in the pose and breathe, allowing the breath to bring new life into the body while staying in the present moment, and reprogram in a new memory.

The other option is the person can take back their power from the memory by choosing to move the body in a way that perhaps they were unable to do during the traumatic event. Either way, with the sensitive guidance of a well-trained trauma-informed instructor, the posture becomes a way to reprogram the nervous system to create a new pathway related to the sensation. What once was a sensation of trauma could become a sensation of power and choice.

The key to being able to sense the body is to understand the nature of our being to feel sensation and right away interpret that sensation with meaning, i.e., "I feel this in my leg and this is why..." This immediately activates the mind, and draws you into a story of either the past or the future.

The breath keeps you present. As the breath becomes more conscious, and you become more in control of your breath, you become more in control of your mind.

As you feel the experience of your body, with the present moment awareness of breath, you create space to notice what is happening within you. This begins a journey of curiosity and exploration. To begin to be with the subtlety of sensation without story is to begin to let go of what was in order to create space for what will be.

I recall an experience during a yoga class where I felt this deep burning in my upper back. Sweat was dripping and my heart was racing. It was the middle of class, intensity in the practice increasing, yet I needed to slow down. After years of practicing, I knew not to push myself. I laid down on my mat. My teacher, attuned to my past through a developed relationship, came over to me to see if I was okay. I explained what was happening, as my legs started shaking. She brought me blankets and two sandbags, asking me to set up in a supported savasana to help my nervous system soothe and relax.

I rested there, just breathing, feeling the support of the ground under me and the familiar sound of her voice as she led others through the rest of the practice. By the time the class ended I was back in regulation and well. This is what happens when you learn to listen to the needs of the body, and not push it past its edge. The edges are there as information and guidance, not as a way to cause harm.

As you begin to feel safe to feel the sensation in your body, over time, with a little more sensation at a time, you can increase your capacity to feel. As you increase your capacity to feel without reacting to the sensation, you are increasing your resilience to stress.

This takes time! Remember, it is not helpful, and can be harmful, to flood the tub. A little drop at a time makes for more resilience.

Please remember that your body, with its amazing intelligence, did exactly what it was supposed to do to keep you safe. That Divine Intelligence, the Holy Spirit, that is alive in you knew what to do, when to do it, how to do it, and it also knows how to help you overcome any residual pain lingering inside. Your body is the temple of God, and it is your birthright to reclaim it and own it as yours. Creating a relationship of compassion, love, and gratitude with your body greatly helps in enjoying your life each day.

CHAPTER TWENTY-TWO

UNDERSTANDING THE POWER OF BREATH

I cannot tell you how many times I was told to, "Breathe. Just take a few deep breaths" during moments of anger or anxiety. I wanted to punch someone which, yes, goes to show you how repressed my issues were, and let's just be honest here, no one ever calms down by telling them to breathe in that moment. In fact, I'm going to suggest that when someone is freaking out, the last thing to tell them to do is to breathe. Invite them to move their body by running in place, shake their body out, or jumping jacks. This will be more helpful in breaking the stress response and get the nervous system back into balance.

The first memory of my breath changing how I felt was in 2006, after my son was born. I was experiencing some pretty intense postpartum symptoms, yet I had no idea what it was at that time.

It was the second day we were home from the hospital. It was nighttime, and I was trying to get some rest as my son slept. My husband was in the living room with guests that had arrived to see our baby.

My body was trembling and shaking, I couldn't calm down and my mind was racing.

In an effort to help myself, I called Kent from my closet floor. He started to do some remote energy work on me and said I needed to get back into my body, not that I knew what that meant. He said the trauma of childbirth, combined with the hormone imbalances that are normal after childbirth, were causing these symptoms. He proceeded to guide me into a meditation where I was breathing into each part of my body, starting with my toes. I wasn't sure about the whole breathing into each part of my body, it was a struggle enough to breathe at all.

Somewhere within that meditation I felt myself calm down. I recall feeling much more peaceful after that. He recommended some herbs to start immediately. What he did not say, though I think he wanted to, was that what I was really experiencing was an upheaval of unprocessed trauma flooding my system, and the childbirth activated it because that's what childbirth does to many women, hence the postpartum depression tendency.

It was just four months after that when I began to practice yoga. Again, the instructor was guiding me in how to breathe at the beginning of practice, during the poses, and at the end. I laughed at the many constant reminders on when to inhale and when to exhale. I also started to realize how often I was not breathing, and instead holding my breath.

As mentioned before, if breath is life, and I was holding my breath, I was holding myself away from that which gives life. How often are you holding your breath and not filing yourself with life?

In the yogic teachings, the breath is the tool that manages the mind. If the breath is steady, the mind is steady. If the breath is frozen, the nervous system has shifted into a faint/freeze response. If the breath is rapid, the nervous system has shifted into a fight/flight response. By learning to attend to and regulate the breath, you are learning how to regulate your nervous system, the intention being that this is a tool you have with you all the time.

Breath work is what I find to be the least utilized tool, and one of the most effective at helping to bring balance and harmony into being. Many breath techniques can be done without anyone knowing you are doing them, and a silent way to find grounding and ease.

The breath is talked about over forty-two times in the Bible. It is referenced as a source of life, as the breath of God, and the gift of life. It is through the breath that we experience the fullness of life. We are so much more capable of managing our internal response than we realize, or give ourselves the opportunity to do so.

Your breath, the source of life within you, the mover of prana, your life force, has the capacity to heal the wounding of the heart, long inflicted by the pains of your past. By learning how to move prana through you, the manifestations of pain caused by the traumas of your past begin to melt into wholeness.

The breath is the vehicle to use, the body is the gateway in, the way your body responds to the triggers is the entrance to information highways taking you within to reclaim a piece of yourself left behind when the pain was too much. The healing you are seeking is found in the pain you are avoiding. There are many ways to enter that pain safely and gently. I find that presence with sensation in the body, gently held by the inhalation and exhalation of breath, combined with compassion and love, begins the process of revealing the light within these spaces of darkness.

When we begin to harness the power of controlling our breath, we begin to activate the power of prana, our Divine intelligence within us, to do the healing needed from the inside out. All that is asked of us is for presence and stillness. It is most often in the stillness that we find the well of healing.

When I entered my yoga teacher training program, the very first thing we were asked to do is to breathe. We were taught a three-part yogic breath, also known as diaphragmatic breathing. It begins to shift the common chest breathing into the diaphragm and abdomen.

The inhalation begins in the belly, rising through the ribcage and into the chest. The exhalation begins in the chest, travels through the ribcage, and completes itself in the lower abdomen. This immediately starts to regulate the nervous system. It is also a common practice suggested by western medicine to help calm anxiety.

Since I was practicing yoga for a few years, this breath practice was very familiar to me, and yet, like most practices in my life at that time, I did not employ them at the right time each day.

For some reason, and I believe this relates back to learned patterns, we may have the tools that could help us in certain situations, yet when the moment arrives that we need a tool, we forget that we have it.

Immediately we turn to the external world, when we really need to attend to the internal world.

Remember, your breath is the tool most accessible and always available at any time.

As the years went on, and my studies in yoga therapy continued, I learned so much about how to watch the breath, how to notice its tendencies, how to use different breath practices at different times to help clients achieve balance and inner harmony. I cannot emphasize enough how I wish I had known this during my early stages of healing:

Even the experience of breath can be a trigger, and if you have not built the capacity to feel sensation safely, you must start very gently and with very little activation. This is why, as mentioned earlier, asking someone who is in a panic response to breathe is not helpful. You must get them to move their body first, for example by running fast in place, to release the surface energy. After that first layer of energy has been released you can then slowly begin to invite them to consciously breathe. After a couple minutes of breathing, you may invite in the simple body awareness of the feet on the ground. The smell in the air. The sounds around them. The things they can see in the room.

Sometimes, and this is very common in trauma healing, being with the sensations in the body doesn't feel safe. As mentioned, this includes noticing the breath and breathing consciously. This is why it is not all about the breath. Remember, there has to be a combination of options available to choose the right tool, the right practice, at the right time.

The breath is the connector between the mental body and the physical body, the bridge between the conscious and unconscious mind. It is our breath that gives us life and our life force is moved through us by the breath. The energy body is equal to the element of water. We are made up of mostly water. This water is malleable, until experiences happen in life that cause a fear response. This fear response, if not attended to, can create a hardening of energy. The once flowing water now turned to ice.

In the Amrit Lineage of yoga, this is referred to as "frozen prana." This prana that is simply trying to flow through you can now become hardened, and every single time something happens that mimics that same energy of the past situation, that "ice" is triggered. This trigger creates physical sensations around the part of the body where the prana is stuck.

This is brilliant wisdom waiting for you. The tendency is to avoid it, numb it, repress it, push it away, when really what we want to learn how to do is be with it from a place of compassion and kindness. It is neither good nor bad, right nor wrong. It simply is.

We can ask ourselves, "Is this the right time for me to do this deep piece of work? Or do I need to create some space in my life to allow myself the time to be present to this healing?"

My therapist would always ask me this before we began any piece of work. It was always my choice. This energy, this water, this prana, is just trying to return to a state of wholeness. It often feels awful inside when it is activated, kind of like a piece of the ice has been chipped away and is scratching your insides. It aches. It is painful. Our ego-mind does not like pain. It does everything it can to avoid pain.

The avoidance of pain is a cause of suffering.

It is only through the pain that you find the gold. That is what is so hard sometimes. Once you learn how you best process, and find the tools that work best for you in a given time, the processing gets a little easier, and you know the steps you need to take, to do what you need to do, for your highest healing.

The energy body is the inner manager, meaning if one disconnects from the physical body the energy has no form to take. Water takes the form of any container, yet without a container, it simply spills everywhere. Our energy is much the same – it needs the safety of the physical body to contain it. If you are disconnected from the physical body due to constant dissociation, it is impossible to manage your energy.

Once you feel safely contained, then transformation can occur. I relate this to a caterpillar going into a cocoon, becoming mush, then reforming into a butterfly. I imagine this is a very painful process, yet a necessary one to become what God created it to be.

Darla once asked me in a therapy session if I was willing to believe that the energy inside of me had the power to heal the pain inside of me.

I said, "Yes. I believe the power of Love that lives inside of me has the power to hold and heal the pain."

She asked, "Are you willing to believe that the pain is not trying to hurt you? It is a part of you waiting for your own love."

Due to my background, I affirmed, "Yes, I believe this. Now how do I help these parts come into wholeness and integrate?"

Her response: "Slowly, and over time."

There is no timeline on healing. Recovery is a lifelong journey with mountains and valleys. As we come to understand the nature of Love, never satisfied until all parts of you are embodied in it, we know that when we are out of balance it's an opportunity to expand our capacity to hold love.

CHAPTER TWENTY-THREE

CALMING THE MIND

The mind can only know what it has always known until you give it new information. When you have thoughts that repeat themselves over and over again, creating a pattern of energy, in order to break that pattern, you must move your body, change your breath, and create new thoughts.

The thinking mind cannot solve a feeling; however, it can be employed to shift a feeling by thinking a new thought. The challenge becomes knowing when to engage the thinking mind instead of the feeling body, and when to focus on the feeling body, not the thinking mind.

The body will always remember what the mind tries so hard to forget. As the body releases the past in the present moment, through the experience of sensation in the body, the mind can be engaged to create a new pattern, a new perception of the past experience, and make meaning out of the pain. This becomes a process of using the mind to create a new story.

All thoughts that you have ever thought were not original thoughts. They were words spoken to you, in front of you or within earshot, on tv, radio, by someone you know or even a stranger. These thoughts were not your own, yet you adopted them to be so. It is only when you begin to take control of your thoughts by identifying as the thinker, not the thought itself, that you can then begin to reprogram your mind to think thoughts that you may never have thought before.

For example, if you were always told, "Don't even try. You won't be good at it," then every time you think about trying something new this thought pattern takes over and you may never even try.

As you consider that perhaps that thought is not true, maybe it is a thought that your parents, teacher, coach, sibling said to you because they were afraid of failure or not being good enough, you begin to realize that you can take back power over your thoughts, that you have a choice. The power to choose your thoughts gives you the ability to create a new life.

When making a decision that aligns with the way you want to live your life, especially if many decisions in the past were made from a space of trauma instead of harmony, it will feel very uncomfortable inside your body.

Remember, your body is the warehouse of all your past experiences and parts of you. I like to compare the body to the cloud on the internet. It stores and backs up data that you cannot see, and even stuff you thought you got rid of. When you feel triggered, oftentimes there is a part of you coming online, like an old program starting to run that you thought you had sent to the trash bin. This part of you may not have the skills or self-agency to well handle the situation. A five-year-old cannot handle the responsibility of an adult, although the child will certainly try.

Making informed choices and feeling like you can decide is part of a healthy adult mind. Knowing that there is not one choice but a multitude of options, all of which present different consequences of both shadow and light, is part of the consideration process.

A traumatized nervous system will activate when faced with a choice, most often due to a freeze response in the past where choice was taken away and doing what others expected and wanted felt "safe," when really we were choosing out of fear. In this situation the person chooses a false sense of survival and continues deepening the groove of trauma.

An integrated being with a healthy nervous system will look at it all and hopefully choose what is most aligned with their Truth, creating a new neural pathway. The reclamation of power from abusive energies of the past creates space for new neural networks to be formed.

The power to choose is a very important part of individuation and autonomy in neurological development and rewiring. When this power is embodied, you feel empowered, not anxious or fearful.

Instead of choicelessness or a codependent-based decision, the integrated being chooses what might feel uncomfortable and even a little edgy due to a new pattern being formed. The edginess becomes a sign of progress, rather than fear.

Just as a muscle that has not been worked for a while gets tender, sore and achy when you finally activate it again, the felt sense of making a new choice, a healthier choice, can often leave that same achy, tender feeling inside.

There comes a point in trauma recovery where you must be more curious about who you are becoming than who and where you have been. While the old pattern may seem comfortable and safe, as the fear you know is more comfortable than the one that is unknown, the new pattern is leading you to expanded horizons and unseen territory.

I recall many moments when simple choices would flood my nervous system out of fear of upsetting other people. I was stuck mentally and physically and often would not be able to speak.

I remember when I was fourteen being in the car with my oldest brother, Barrett, and his then girl-friend, and now sister-in-law, going to get lunch. They asked me where I wanted to go.

I said, "I don't care."

They asked again. I replied with the same answer.

They asked again, saying that they were not going to go any-where until I told them where I wanted to go, both genuinely wanting to take me somewhere of my choosing.

I froze. I was in the back seat and couldn't think straight. After what felt like many minutes I named a local burger place.

I always wondered why I froze. Why was it so hard to make a simple choice? It was a trauma response. This was not a traumatic experience – they were taking me to lunch and simply wanted me to choose – but to my nervous system, wired on trauma, it felt like my safety was threatened.

I was so scared of choosing somewhere they would not like – and, in my mind, maybe not love me because of that choice — that I froze up and had no voice. That's what trauma response does in a simple way. It doesn't have to make sense.

As I got older and had similar experiences, I realized how so many of my decisions were based on pleasing others and out of fear of what they would think.

I knew I was starting to make a big shift in my healing journey when I began to care more about what I thought than about what anyone else said or could think about my decision. I started to choose based on what was in alignment with my values, instead of what supported another person's desire or even what they wanted me to choose so they didn't have to deal with their own emotional upset.

Each time I did this, it became a little easier inside. I learned how to make healthy choices from a place of worthiness and boundaries. Each time I was faced with a decision that I knew could disappoint another, I asked myself:

What decision is going to help me move closer to the life I am co-creating with God?

Is this choice coming from self-love or fear of their disapproval?

Is this choice going to lead me closer to peace or pull me farther away from it?

How does it feel in my body and what does that feeling want me to know?"

In yoga, we can use the postures to help create new choices by experiencing different sensations in the body, and choosing how intense or gentle to make the pose. We can choose to shift the breath to change the process of the mind, thereby shifting the emotional energy.

We can employ the philosophy to help understand how the old choices create more suffering and the new choice, while it may feel uncomfortable, by using the awareness of "I am not the discomfort. I am the one experiencing it and therefore have the power to change it" we create a new level of consciousness about any situation.

The teachings and practices of yoga gave me the tools to feel strong enough to make new choices. EMDR helped to reprogram my nervous system into a response of options instead of codependent fear. The two together allowed me to learn how to choose based on self-love.

As therapy continued through 2018, I kept working with parts of myself that were so relieved to finally be seen, heard, and held in love. My therapy shifted to learning how to think in a new way. I had to resource myself through books, mentors, friends who think differently than I do, to help me find new thoughts to program into my mind and heart.

I chose to use the Bible as my main resource for healthy thinking, focusing on who God says I am, as well as several books in

psychotherapy, neuroscience, and neurological and psychological development for childhood milestones. When your mind has
always been ruled by shame, it takes commitment, mindfulness,
and awareness to consciously choose a new thought.

It is not as easy as wiping a computer clean from old software.
The deleting of mental files takes a long time, and reprogramming just the same. As I used resources to reprogram my mind,
I became more aware of other programs running in my mind/
body/heart complex that also needed to be rewired.

My faith informed me that even if someone is upset with me, I
am not responsible for their reaction. My faith also informed me
that others are allowed to be upset with me, and I can be okay even
if someone is mad at me. I was sitting in meditation one morning,
struggling with the constant concern over what others thought of
me. This is a program that had been running in my mind and heart
for far too long. I had my Bible out with me, as I had previously
done some devotional reading prior to meditating. I heard God
say, "Open to Galatians. Start at the beginning."

I had never read Galatians. In fact, I was not even sure if it was
a book in the Bible. I knew by that point to listen to that guidance.
It never steered me wrong. I opened my Bible.

I came to this verse:

"Am I now trying to win the approval of human beings, or of
God?" (Galatians 1:10, NIV[8])

I think that made it very clear. I laughed out loud. Thanks, God.
I surrendered my fear of what other people thought of me, really
a fear of abandonment and rejection, to God that day. I continue
to surrender it every time I make a choice. Every time I feel inad-
equate. Every time I feel that I am not enough.

This verse replays in my mind. I no longer live my life in concern of what others think; I live my life in accordance with what I

promised God. My mind is continually being reprogrammed into a mindset of strength and possibility; releasing fear-based beliefs and shame-filled buckets of false truths about who I am.

I don't freeze very often anymore. Sometimes I find myself waiting to feel if I do, then I smile in gratitude for the gift of resilience. I bounce back from stress exponentially faster than in the past. What used to trigger me is no longer causing suffering. That is not a miracle. That is the result of consistent inner work.

The mind and emotions are not identifiable truths. They are constantly changing based upon perceptions of daily experiences. By learning to observe thoughts and notice emotion, you become more capable of navigating stressful situations.

This space creates a deeper awareness of the energy of Love that is always behind the scenes. If my thoughts don't align with God's Truths, then they are not thoughts that serve me. When my mind and my emotions are anchored in Truth, in Love, I am more resilient.

I often ask myself, "Is this thought Holy?" meaning a thought aligned with who God says I am, or "Is this thought unholy?" meaning based on a lie I was taught, told, modeled, or adopted. I chose to train myself and continue to do so, to think Holy thoughts; thoughts that are rooted in Truth and Love. The mind can be tamed and trained. It is necessary to do this once the body has processed the unresolved pain.

CHAPTER TWENTY-FOUR

EMOTIONAL EMBODIMENT: FEEL IT TO FREE IT

What parts of yourself have you quarantined for so long that every time they cause a disruption to your life you add another lock on the cage? I asked myself this question in a meditation years ago. It was intense and enlightening. These shadows are not parts of you to be caged, thrown away, disowned, ashamed of, killed off, left behind, saged away, thrown into the fire. These are not demons or the enemy lurking inside of you.

These are tender, precious parts of you, seeking to be seen, heard, held, loved. When it is the right time, you will begin to invite the sacredness of compassionate holding into each of these parts, just as you longed for as a child. They reside within your body, causing aching, painful sensations to get your attention.

If you will be with them one by one, taking the locks off the cage and giving these parts space to share their story, their hurts, their needs. You will discover they held the key to your freedoms all along, and they have been waiting for you to set yourself free. As you embrace each part, you understand the purpose and passion they bring in your life.

You will eventually integrate them into wholeness. When the time comes that they seek your love, you will open the door, and listen. Just be with these parts of you. They are what you have been seeking. Your own love.

There is a great misunderstanding of emotions as they are often presented as bad or in comparison with their opposite emotion. For example, anger is often labeled as bad and happiness is labeled as good. I think it is fair to say that there is a right place for anger to emerge, as in when a child is sexually abused. I think it is fair to say that one would have a right to be rage-filled at times.

The emotion itself is not a problem. The emotion is energy moving through the human body, causing a neural response that we then label as emotions based on a collection of symptoms that most relate to a prior experience when we felt the same way.

Anxiety presents with a myriad of symptoms, often the same symptoms for each individual. One person may have a heavy chest, while another feels like their throat is closing. Another may have a pain in their stomach, while another loses sense of grounding. When I teach yoga therapy for anxiety workshops, I ask the participants to share their physical symptoms of anxiety. A list of fifty-plus symptoms are typically shared, all labeled as anxiety.

None of these symptoms are wrong. In fact, when followed therapeutically with a skilled practitioner, it is these very symptoms that become the gateways to integration and healing.

The key to healing is being able to stay present to the sensations of emotions as they present as physical sensations. The emotional energy and their corresponding symptoms are not trying to hurt you. They are trying to capture your attention to nurture a part of you left behind a long time ago. In order to heal from trauma, you must learn how to be with uncomfortable sensations in your body.

When you begin to invite love to wake up inside you, it searches for all the ways you have built walls against it. Love seeks itself over and over again. It will not settle for anything less than one hundred percent fullness. This means that all the stories, the lies, the messages, and the inner voice telling you that you aren't good enough, or unworthy, or scared, or stupid, or ugly, or dumb, or so many other awful things that you would never say to a small child, need to be held in love and brought into wholeness. Each of these parts of you present as the sensations of emotions in your body.

The teachings of yoga state that:

1. *Yoga happens in the NOW.*
2. *Yoga is the stilling (calming and clearing) of the fluctuations of the mind*
3. *So that the Seer (you) can abide (rest deeply) in its own true nature (which is love).*

Jesus says:

1. *Be still and know.*
2. *I have given you a spirit of power, of a sound, clear mind, and of love.*
3. *Remember who you are – with a list of verses that define who you are in God's image.*

The obstacles on the path of love are the ego's invitation for you to free it from its unrecognized pain, from remembering this Truth. In fact, the obstacles *are* the path, meaning, they are not trying to stop you. They are asking to be made new and embraced in love. In order to overcome the pain of the past, you actually need the obstacle to make you aware of the blocked energy.

Emotions and the sensations created from the energy are intentional to help you. Yes, you will fight it. Yes, you will reject it at times. Yes, you will continue to meet all the parts of you seeking your love and God's love until every part is welcomed home. That is the beauty of love. It will not stop searching for its missing pieces until every last one is home.

A spiritual journey isn't enchanting and fantastical in its mystical moments. A spiritual journey is choosing to go to battle for yourself every day until you remember who you are as love. The warrior of light within you is battling for a sacred promise – its commitment is to fight for love over and over again until you are standing fully in the glory that God designed for your life. A spiritual journey is completely embracing your humanity.

Your emotions are the messengers you need to become intimate with life, to experience God's design for your life so fully that you are filled with Spirit. Emotions give information providing an explanation for how your nervous system is perceiving an event, experience, or person. The emotions are not meant to be states of being; they are meant to be your nervous system's way of sharing with you how it feels about something. Those feelings are to give you insight and awareness as to what is needed in that experience to bring safety and regulation. The feelings create body-based sensations that you will label as the emotion itself.

For example: Your nervous system is perceiving a situation as overwhelming. This results in the label of anxiety. It is experienced as heart-racing, sweaty palms, upset stomach, headache, tight throat, restricted breathing.

Ideally this would provide insight that either you need to leave the situation, find a different approach to it, change your perception of it, or seek support from someone else who has the ability to stay calm and steady. Depending on your past experiences with this energy of overwhelm, the body reacts or responds in the way that is most programmed.

Learning to use the power of presence through breath and sensational awareness, you can begin to reprogram your capacity to stop the stress response and create a new neural pathway of conscious decisions.

A stress interrupter, the practice of breathing and/or naming what is happening in the present moment, provides the space to discern if there is danger or if your nervous system is reacting from an emotional flashback. As you learn to understand emotions as information giving explanation, you gain deeper knowledge on how to best support yourself in times of stress. Emotional intelligence becomes a refined skill, and emotions become a great source of wisdom.

Harvard Brain Scientist Jill Bolte Taylor says in her book, *My Stroke of Insight*, "When a person has a reaction to something in their environment, there's a ninety-second chemical process that happens in the body; after that, any remaining emotional response is just the person choosing to stay in that emotional loop."[8]

This means that for ninety seconds, if you can feel the sensations of emotions, without going into a story about what you are feeling, you have the ability to break the stress cycle in the body/ mind complex.

It is the story created about the sensation that causes the sensation to linger. If there is trauma being activated in the nervous system, there may be an unconscious reaction alerting the system that safety is not secured.

In this situation, the only goal is cultivating regulation and safety. This can be done in several ways, the most important is present-moment awareness.

The following is a practice I enjoy using for myself. It involves anchoring into the present moment by using the breath and sensory experience that is safe for you.

Left hand on heart, Right hand on belly.

I slow way down inside, as if turning a volume control from high to low.

Eyes open, I begin to breathe, filling my abdomen into my right hand, and guiding my breath up into my heart under my left hand.

As I exhale, I feel the breath softening into my heart, and releasing all the way down to my lower abdomen.

I notice what is around me as I am breathing.

I make mental notes of what I see, what I can hear, what I can smell.

I mentally remind myself that in that very moment, I am safe.

I do this until I feel a shift inside, a presence of peace returning.

While the mind will often try to forget the past, the body never will. That said, by using integrative practices, you can reprogram the nervous system, which will then help to rewire the mind. The body must clear the trauma, the mind must learn new programs. The two eventually work together for harmony. Emotional intelligence is a necessary skill to succeed in creating a harmonious life.

Emotions are messengers of experienced life. They are not meant to cause suffering. They are meant to make you aware of your experience of life, and how your nervous system is receiving said situation. As you learn to label the emotion, notice the associated sensations within the body, allow the part of you holding the experience to be held in Love, the story that causes suffering will begin to fade. What is left is the wisdom of the soul.

Mother Mary came to me in a session sharing this message: "Kate, your worth is not dependent on the ever-changing conditions of being human. You are worthy because you are a child of God. Your soul is holding the records of all the lives you have lived. This life you are living is the culmination of all the past experiences and opportunity to overcome generational pain and oppression by learning to walk in the light of Christ Consciousness. This light lives in each soul on Earth. When it activates, its intention is to call forth all the parts of you lost in time and bring them into the radiant well of light alive within the heart. This light in the heart is the embodiment of Christ. As you embody this light, you are able to meet another as a soul, walking in the Holiness of being human. Your humanity is a gift, Kate. Use it well."

CHAPTER TWENTY-FIVE

THE WISDOM OF THE HEART

In 2012 during a dream, I was with a team of three other people, and we were on a mission to help rescue others locked in a building. They were being held hostage.

This was the third "installation" of a continuous dream over a few nights. I was on a Warrior team, and we're finishing up our training. This was one of our final missions.

As we entered the building, I saw many people in a room. We talked with them and continued in through another door, a flight of stairs, and entered another room. This continued for three floors.

I did not see any people holding them hostage. There was no exit to the building. I don't know how we got in; it was almost as if we'd been transported. Finally I asked the people why they were there. The responses were that they had all their needs provided for, and just couldn't get out. They'd tried for many years, and just kept finding walls and doors.

I looked up at the walls. There were tiny windows lining the top of the wall where it met the ceiling.

I climbed on a table and broke the windows. The words I said will stick with me forever:

"Sometimes you have to look to the window within to find your way out."

All the people in that building climbed out, some with hesitance of what life would be like if they were free, each seeing the outside world in a new way and having a choice of how they moved forward.

The ancient yogic text, The Upanishads, states "There is a light that shines beyond all things on earth, beyond us all, beyond the heavens, beyond the highest, the very highest heavens. This is the radiant light that shines in the heart of man."[9] It is said that when we surrender to that light, we are resting in our wholeness.

The Bible talks about the light of the heart, which the Holy Spirit inhabits and uses to renew the heart. It is where the Holy Spirit makes you whole in spirit. Neuroscientists discovered how the heart has more neural networking and memory than the brain. It is only through the healing of the heart, via the vagus nerve, that the whole being integrates.

The heart is the deepest place of wisdom within us and the highest intellect, our intuition. It is where we remember our wholeness. It is the essence of Truth that lives alive within you and travels through the physical body as subtle energy, guiding you all the time. It is the energy of love trying to let you know when something is right for you or when something is wrong for you. It is the wisdom of the Holy Spirit directing your steps each day.

The Wisdom Body, as it is called in the yogic teachings, is fueled by discernment, and the deeper understanding of how life is interacting with you and through you. There is a misconception that intuition is woo-woo and New Age. This is far from the truth. All the great teachers speak about this higher intellect as a source of wisdom. It is formed within our physical body in heightened senses, beyond the physical realm. These senses are often overly developed in someone with a lot of trauma, as a means of keeping them safe in daily life.

I have spent many years teaching others about intuitive development, and how to reclaim a relationship to this part of themselves. As I journeyed through recovery, I came to learn how this connection can also be used to disconnect from the physical body, creating a deeper groove for dissociation. Even with this knowledge, I was uneducated on the brilliance of our energy body to heighten the gifts of the Spirit in an attempt to help survive human suffering. The experience of Spirit is much more powerful inside of you than outside of you.

I took a lot of time studying the psychology of the chakras, and the connections between energetic development and the nervous system. I also studied how Christ's teachings exactly align with the developments of the chakras.

I learned that when the nervous system developed in trauma, the lower two chakras that are ideally developed in safety and connection – with the right to be here and feel all of life through our senses – instead developed in fear of life, lack of security, and a disconnect from the Authentic Self due to unprocessed emotional experiences.[10]

This disconnect causes miswiring in the body/mind complex, leading to an overdevelopment of mistrust in other humans, and a need to develop another way to survive unhealthy and unsafe situations.

The intuitive senses begin to overdevelop to keep the person safe. This means that just as an octopus uses its tentacles to feel, the human uses its energy senses to feel, instead of the human emotional functions. The problem becomes that a child has no means to know how to manage these heightened gifts.

The wisdom that is meant to develop from life experiences is now clouded with the wounding of the past. The intuition that is meant to help keep someone safe is now layered with the wounding that is too intense to process.

When someone self-labels as highly empathic to the point where they absorb another's pain, what they are really saying is they have overdeveloped their clairsentient intuitive gift to be able to create a sense of safety within them. The empathic gift of sensing what another is experiencing was used to become almost chameleon-like to help the empath feel safe in their environment, to fit in because they don't feel like they belong.

What this causes is a misidentification of the sense versus the wisdom. What is meant to help you is actually causing an internal disconnect with the guidance inside of you, and leading you to believe that by feeling someone else's pain you will be more safe in the world.

The trauma becomes mislabeled as Truth, and when something in life starts to match the energy of the past pain, the nervous system interprets it as Truth, when it is really a false sense of safety.

This can even lead to a dissociative state of being, where it is hard to connect to reality or where you feel foggy, panicky, unable to feel your physical body, disconnected to your internal needs like hunger, thirst, bathroom urges, sleep. It could also present as nightmares, hallucinations, being overly compassionate to the point that it causes you suffering, a shutdown of any spiritual connection, and even a desire to leave this physical realm.

These wounds intertwine with neural development and there is nothing you did to cause it to happen. It happened to help you live. The good news is that the nervous system is able to be reprogrammed, and the overdeveloped intuition can be reprogrammed into healthy discernment. The reprogramming of the past pain, by processing the blocked emotional energy, allows for Truth to begin to flow deep inside. You will no longer be led by shame, fear, and guilt.

How do you know it is Truth? It will align with love, compassion, grace, mercy, patience, gentleness, worthiness, healing, wholeness. The Truth will reflect who God says you are; not who the lies of the past made you believe yourself to be.

The wisdom begins to overtake the wounding.

The overdeveloped senses begin to integrate and calm as the intellect of discerning wisdom starts to grow. Your nervous system begins to collect the data from the past while filtering out the pain, and a regeneration of life starts to bloom inside.

This regeneration is shown in science as the growth of the ends of your DNA strands, or telomeres. Yes, you have the power to regenerate and create new life inside of you! The past does not define you, and when given the safe, healthy environments needed, your body can heal itself, just as God designed you to do. Science calls this epigenetics – the ability to change our DNA.

This Wisdom Body reminds me directly of the gift of the Holy Spirit. We are given new life inside of us when we embody Christ.

While in one of my early EMDR sessions, the intent was to connect to my teenage self who was often angry and wanting to run away from all responsibilities in life. While she had good reason, she was often the part of me causing myself a lot of suffering.

The session started by me entering my body at my right hip.

Jesus appeared right away in my vision and showed me myself at seventeen – angry, scared, mad at life. He also showed my six-year-old self, shaking in fear, terrified, and alone. He said to me, "This is how you see your past and you. I understand. Horrible things happened to you that justify the pain. However, Kate, let me show you what I see."

He proceeded to show me myself at six shining in the light, joyous, bright, laughing, with various happy memories flashing through my psyche. He showed me my seventeen-year-old self having fun, smart, beautiful, praised and loving life. He showed me my life full of joy and love.

He said, "Kate, your pains no longer define you. I have carried you through it all and I will forever be by your side. It is time to embody joy and let love in your heart. Let Me show you something more."

He showed me a six-pointed star, like the Star of David. My two six-year-old selves were at the left side points, my two seventeen-year-old selves were at the right two sides. My lower self was at the bottom. My higher self was at the top. Jesus was in the middle.

"It is going to spin now," He said, "It will be okay." The image started spinning. I recall feeling like I was being unwound and reprogrammed into peace. When the image stopped, Jesus was at the top of the star and Mother Mary was at the bottom. I was in the middle and my aspects of self were there smiling.

"You weren't ready to understand until now. When you came back into this world, Mother Mary brought My light with you and through you. As she helped bring you back, you and I became one. Her love lives in you. My grace and spirit flow through you now. It is time for you to be who you came back to be. These pains have to be processed out of your nervous system to create more space for light and grace. Remember, I am you. You are Me. We are one. Be the light. It is time."

I recalled a Bible verse that says:

"No one has ever seen God; but if we love one another, God lives in us and His love is made complete in us." (1 John 4:12, NIV.)

All this was happening with my eyes open, tracking lights and holding tappers as my therapist held the space and kept me anchored in the sensations in my body.

I asked Him why He moved positions in the star. He said, "Because it is time for you to take your rightful place within yourself. You are whole. You have always been whole. You simply forgot. You are the light of Christ, sent here in this Sacred Vessel to share the teachings of compassion with the world. Go do this in memory of Me. I am always with you."

I was in tears. It was all so surreal yet just as real as if we were sitting in the room together having a conversation.

This is when I knew that trauma, when given the right support, can be utilized for great spiritual understanding and deep wisdom. Everyone has the light of Christ within them, and it has nothing to do with religion. It has to do with an inner relationship with the Light of Love that breathes alive in you all the time. It is often activated in times of great suffering, as the ego cannot control things any longer.

The wisdom of understanding Truth, of embodying it, of allowing it to wire like a new program being installed into a computer, changes your entire system, your DNA, your life.

You have access to this wisdom. Everyone has access to it. You are the Light of Christ. Yes, you. This light is the light that illuminates the world. This light is the light that radiates love. This light is the light of hope that can eradicate all fear. It lives alive in you right now. No one, no situation, no trauma can take that away from you. It is an innate part of you that birthed in you upon the first beat of your heart. When we access this wisdom, there is nothing to fear. We become that which we have been seeking, Love.

If you are willing to follow the sensations in the body to unwind the pain of the past, you will be given the keys to unlock the doors to ancient wisdom held within the cellular structure of your being. The heart holds the key to wholeness.

We begin to remember our wholeness and reclaim the promises made upon incarnating in this body. This wisdom becomes the connective force of light and love, much like a lighthouse always shining to call the ships home. This light of wisdom alive within each of us is always seeking us to return home.

This wisdom is the Highest Intellect, an internal transmission of Truth embodied in your humanity. It is through our humanity that we are able to be the expression of Christ. It is through the complete embodiment of this light that we remember our wholeness, and walk free in this plane of humanity. This doesn't mean we won't experience suffering. It does mean that when suffering comes, we are no longer identified by it as we know and live the Truth of who we are – Love.

While the wounded heart seeps in pain, the wisdom of the heart is a healing balm of grace, compassion, presence, and love. The trauma does dissolve. The memory fades. It becomes subtle, and while you won't forget, you will be free.

Chapter Twenty-Six

DAILY MOMENTS OF BLISS

As I began to walk in wisdom, I was blessed with moments of bliss. The bliss I felt even in moments of despair helped me to understand the totality of our human experience. We are meant to feel it all, yet not identify with any of it. Bliss comes when we can rest in the experience as it is, without needing it to be any different. We have the capacity to hold both the beauty and the pain.

The ocean and the waves are one. The wave is a manifestation of the ocean in her totality. Each wave is a significant expression of the ocean. Each wave is perfect in its own right. I don't believe the ocean ever says to the waves, "You are too small. You are too weak. You are not a good enough wave."

No, the ocean does not say that. The ocean is the unlimited potential of our Truth, manifesting in many various formations throughout our lifetime. The ocean is the Divine Mother, simply waiting for all of her waves to return home. When a wave gets stuck in time, frozen, as discussed earlier, the ocean doesn't leave the wave. She doesn't stop waiting for the return. In fact, the ocean stays there, gently holding that wave until it is ready to return to the well of love from which it came.

This is who you are. You are the ocean and the waves. You are the embodiment of Love in all of its magnificence and in all of its many manifestations.

The bliss of understanding that you have the capacity within you to remember that you are the ocean, and you are the wave, is one of the greatest gifts God gave to being human. You have the choice, the Higher Intellect within you to make choices to create a life you love.

Enlightenment is not being free from the effects of being human. This is my definition of enlightenment: being able to hold space for all the human parts of yourself through the grace of God's love, knowing that in your humanity you are sacred and precious. It is being able to feel it all and not identify with any of it.

While yes, God – The Divine Father and Mother – has the final say on the original plan, you do get to decide how you navigate this life. The bliss that is spoken of in the yogic teachings refers to the ability to notice all aspects of self – the physical body, the energy body, the mental/emotional body, the wisdom body, and even the bliss body – and surrender it all to the Light of Love that lives in your heart. From that place, you can then take the next right action at the right time.

This means that true contentment comes when you are conscious, aware, and able to be present in your body, experience your breath, notice your thoughts, feel your emotions, tune into the wisdom, and rest into bliss. This is the peace that surpasses all understanding. This is the ultimate grace of God – to be one with your humanity, and fully aware of your Divinity, experiencing all of life through the eye of the heart.

This eye, as shown in Mother Mary's *hamseh*, or palm facing outward, is the spiritual eye of the heart (the hand being a mirror of our heart), where we are able to live life from our soul's experience and claim the full inheritance of God's goodness.

"*I pray that the light of God will illuminate the eyes of your imagination, flooding you with light, until you experience the full revelation of the hope of his calling – that is, wealth of God's glorious inheritances that he finds in us, his holy ones.*" (Ephesians 1:18 TPT.)

In this translation, it is said that the "calling" is another name for the innermost heart.[11] And it is through the body that we come to understand the fullness of potential that we were designed to live in this life. The activations of traumas in the nervous system have the capacity to lead you into the highest Truths with you, when you are willing to be with the sensational experience of life happening within you, leading you home.

Bliss, Love, Joy, Peace – this who you are. Your own light will not stop seeking you until all parts are welcomed home. Daily experiences have the potential to move you in and out of this bliss state. Moments in time when you smile and laugh, when time stands still in joy, when you see something differently than once before. A miracle in a moment experienced in your heart.

CHAPTER TWENTY-SEVEN

WHO GOD SAYS YOU ARE

There is gold to be found hidden in the darkness of the past, presenting as symptoms in the now. This gold is worth the dig. It is worth the shaking, the trembling, the three steps forward and two steps back. It is worth the fight and struggle.

Remember that you are not walking alone. You are always held, supported, loved and cared for by the light of Christ that lives in you. God uses people every day to be His walking light for help. There were so many people sent on my path to be the Hope of God in times when I wanted to give up. There is no shame in seeking the support that you need to overcome a painful past.

The bravest thing we could ever do is say the words, "I need help. Please help me."

You are worthy of seeking the right kind of care for you, and continuing to seek that care until you consistently feel whole in your daily life.

I wrote these words in 2018 after returning from a yoga therapy continuing education training. I was deeply feeling the lies that I had believed my entire life about who I am.

"They said to lose weight. I worked out a lot. They said to cover dark circles. I learned the art of makeup. They said

to wear black. I learned the magic of invisibility. They said I couldn't. I learned to be a workaholic. They said I wasn't good enough. I learned I had to prove myself. They said she was prettier. I learned that looks matter more than being smart. They said I had to be quiet and no one cared. I learned to silence my voice and please everyone else. They said not to tell. I learned to live in fear.

I learned I wasn't broken. You told me I am whole.

I learned I wasn't unworthy. You told me I am good enough.

I learned I wasn't ugly. You told me I am beautiful.

I learned my voice mattered. You told me to speak the truth.

I learned I am more than a face. You told me I'm Your child.

I learned I have a purpose. You told me I was given special gifts.

I learned I am loved. You told me I am Yours.

I learned I am just like You. You told me I am perfectly made in Your image.

The choice to listen to You, to live in joy, to walk in love, has given me the grace to write a new story. To love myself. To be brave. To be the light. To act with compassion and kindness. To speak up for those who are suffering. To treat each other with love."

While walking this healing journey I chose to learn the Truth of who I am in reflection of what scripture says about me. I share this with you as a source of remembrance, as a reconnection to the Truth of who you are and who you were long before any of the pain held you hostage.

A powerful list to remind yourself of the
Truth of Who You Are to God.
Allow these words to repeat in your mind.

I am ...

Loved	Jeremiah 31:3
Unique	Psalm 139:13-16
Precious	1 Cor 6:20
Adopted	Ephesians 1:5
Wonderfully Made	Psalm 139:14
His	Isaiah 43:1
Renewed	2 Cor 4:16
Held	Colossians 1:17
Lavished in Love	1 John 3:1
Important	1 Peter 2:9
Forgiven	Psalm 103:12
Protected	Psalm 121:3
Chosen	John 15:16
Free	Colossians 2:11
Strong	Psalm 68:35
Special	Ephesians 2:10
Empowered	Phil 4:13
Beautiful	Psalm 45:11
Created in His image	Genesis 1:27
Accepted	Romans 15:7
Worthy	Isaiah 43:1
A New Creation	2 Cor 5:17
Created for a purpose	Jeremiah 29:11

Lovely	Daniel 12:3
Family	Ephesians 2:19
Rescued	Colossians 1:13
Known	Psalm 139:1
Saved	Ephesians 2:4-5
Healed	Psalm 147:3
Blessed	Ephesians 1:3
A Child of God	1 John 3:1
Transformed	2 Cor 3:18
Victorious	Romans 8:37
Radiant	Matthew 5:14
Pursued	Psalm 23:6
Valuable	Luke 12:7
Wanted	2 Peter 3:9
Courageous	Deuteronomy 31:6
Redeemed	Romans 3:24
Gifted	James 1:17
Bold	2 Cor 3:12
Masterpiece	Ephesians 2:10
Never Alone	Deuteronomy 31:8
Whole	& Complete Colossians 2:10
Delighted In	Zephaniah 3:17
Belong	1 Cor 6:20
A temple of God	1 Cor 3:16
Friend	John 15:15
Justified	Romans 3:22-24
Worth it	Romans 5:6-8
Favored	Proverbs 8:35

Joyful	John 15:11
A Daughter of the King	Galatians 3:26
More than Makeup and Clothes	1 Peter 3:3-4
Worth more than Rubies	Proverbs 31:10
Rooted	Colossians 2:6-7
Comforted	John 14:16-18
Safe	1 John 5:18
Delivered	Colossians 1:13
God's Heir	Galatians 4:7
Right in God's Eyes	Romans 5:1
Not Condemned	Romans 8:1-2
Cannot be separated from God's Love	Romans 8:38-39
More than a Conqueror	Romans 8:37
Provided For	Phil 4:19
Treasured	Deuteronomy 7:6
A Child of Light	1 Thess 5:5
Confident	Romans 8:28
Stabile	2 Timothy 1:7
Salt and Light of the Earth	Matthew 5:13-14
Sustained	Isaiah 46:4
Carried	Isaiah 46:4
Supported	Isaiah 41:10

Use this list anytime you get stuck in a story that is full of lies. Remind yourself of who you really are. Embody these words. Feel them into your body through sensations. This is who you were created to be. (Be sure to check out the Connect with Kate page at the end of this book for a bonus gift.)

CHAPTER TWENTY-EIGHT

I AM STRONG ENOUGH NOW, GOD. THANKS.

There were many days when I wanted to quit, when I wanted to give up, when I just didn't feel like I had what it takes to keep going through these weekly sessions of the deepest, hardest work. One time, when I was ready to call and cancel therapy, I heard a voice from within say to me, "Kate, if you give up, if you give in, he wins. They all win. They have taken so much joy and life from you already. Do not let them win!"

This inner strength did not come from me. It came from a force of Love alive within me that knew without any doubt that I was strong. That I could overcome. That I was able to get through this pain, and rebuild my life on the promises of God.

I had all the tools. They stopped working. Thousands of hours of training in ancient practices that were designed to help this very pain were not enough. I surrendered into the Truth that our ego does not have the capacity to overcome trauma.

I didn't want to forgive. I knew I needed to for my own freedom. I wanted to hate. I wanted to be angry. My livelihood and the future of my family were at stake. Choosing to begin to forgive was the moment my healing accelerated. The forgiveness had nothing to do with the other people who hurt me, and everything to do with freeing my heart, my soul, my body, and my mind, for the lingering pain of the past.

The Radiant Light of Love, the Light of Christ, that lives alive within each of us, when awakened, can absolutely overcome any and all acts of hurt thrown against us. Where the enemy wants to destroy, Love breathes life into us. When we allow this life to breathe, healing happens.

I started to use the mantra:

I am happy. I am healthy. I am healed. I am whole.

I would use this all day long. It became a new program running in my mind. When any intrusive thoughts found their way into my heart, these words would take over like someone inside my mind had changed the record in the jukebox in my brain.

I also started learning certain scriptures that would bring me immediately out of the darkest caverns of my past, my favorite being Phil 4:4-9:

Rejoice in the Lord always. I will say it again: Rejoice! Let your gentleness be evident to all. The Lord is near. Do not be anxious about anything, but in every situation, by prayer and petition, with thanksgiving, present your requests to God. And the peace of God, which transcends all understanding, will guard your hearts and your minds in Christ Jesus. Finally, brothers and sisters, whatever is true, whatever is noble, whatever is right, whatever is pure, whatever is lovely, whatever is admirable — if any-thing is excellent or praiseworthy — think about such things. Whatever you have learned or received or heard from me, or seen in me — put it into practice. And the God of peace will be with you.

I wrote this out and memorized it quickly. It became an armor of peace in my mind. These two intentional mental changes began the arduous journey of reprogramming my mind and heart.

When I asked God to make me strong in January of 2016, I was completely unaware that the journey that would unfold would lead into the deepest Love, the most Light, the greatest strength imaginable, and expand my heart's capacity for understanding the nature of human suffering, and why it is so hard at times to overcome. This strength is never-ending and all-enduring. It is the strength of Love, of God's Love. Nothing and no one is stronger.

This is why being a beacon of hope and an embodiment of Christ's love are the daily intentions I live by when I wake up. I fail at times, and I have learned the power of grace, compassion and forgiveness for myself and others. When we choose to walk in the light, as the light, we are giving permission for others to remember their wholeness. We are giving grace for being human.

I genuinely believe that people are doing the best they can with the tools and programming they learned. While the desire to want people to change may never fade, the compassionate knowing that their pain is not my responsibility softens any sting.

One of the greatest acts of Love is to walk with someone in their pain. While I cannot take away your pain, as you need it to climb out of the dark, I can walk with you in it, hold your hand through it, and provide rays of hope as you become your own greatest hero with the help of the greatest Love of all.

Love is a verb, and in the recovery journey the acts of love create a space of safety. It doesn't always require intense processes or mystical experiences. It does require safety, compassion, presence, grace, and love. This is the real magic – being able to meet all of yourself in love.

I chose life in 1999, again in 2016, and each day since.

I chose not just to breathe, but to breathe life, and live well. I did not want to be a soul afraid of dying, or afraid of being hurt. I wanted to be an embodied soul, free to live!

It was not going to be enough for me to just survive this pain. I knew I was going to thrive. I knew deep down within my soul that I was well.

While I was in the integration phase of a therapy session, Jesus said to me, "Kate, you will show them how to overcome this diagnosis, and you will teach them how to do it. Show them how to live and live well."

I have lived the past five years of my life doing just this. Why? Because when I was dead and in-between worlds I made a promise to God. I promised to help others remember their light, and guide them to embody it, and share it with the world. Your unique light is needed. Your light may be the light that helps another find hope in times of darkness and despair. Your light may just be the answer to someone's prayer.

While this story is far from over, and more will be shared, the deeper understanding and promise is that with faith, hope, and love all is possible. I chose to find the purpose in my pain, and it was worth the battle to remember Truth. God will always work things out for good for those who believe. Faith is believing what you cannot yet see.

The recovery journey may not be the way you want it, and it will take time. If you choose to focus on the Love that lives alive within you, you will be carried through the pain with more ease, held through the tears, and delivered from the suffering. Resilience is birthed through consistent care and intentional living.

While we were never promised a life without pain, we are promised peace beyond understanding no matter what pain is present in life.

You have the right to claim this peace!

You have a right to enjoy your life fully and completely with joy and love.

Your Divine birthrights were planted in you from the very beginning, and I pray you will not settle for a life half-lived.

You were made for greatness! You were created with the finest details of attention and intention to fulfill a purpose here far beyond what you might imagine it to be.

You have the power within you to become what you were always designed to be — a sacred embodiment of the greatest Love of all.

You are capable. You are strong. You can handle this, and when you feel like you can't, Love can.

There is hope for healing. It lives inside your radiant heart, and is seeking your love.

You are already whole. You have simply forgotten.

It is time to make the journey home to embody your light and remember your wholeness.

It is my prayer that you will find the courage and boldness to never settle for anything less than reclaiming the promises Love made to you upon soulful embodiment in this life; that love that is constantly seeking you from inside your own heart.

May there come a day when you can say,

"I am strong enough now, God. Thanks. Thank you for it all."

I looked in the books.
I looked in the mountains.
I looked in the woods.
I looked in the ocean.
I looked at the stars.
I traveled the lands seeking the answers.
I asked teachers.

I talked with friends.
I went to doctors.
I sought out healers.
I took the medicine.
I read the scriptures.
I chased the moon.
I burned the letters.
I sweat the pain.
I sat in meditation.
I did the poses.
I talked with my guides.
I burned the sage.
I chanted, sang, cried, and cried some more.
I raged, I released, I breathed.
Finally I stopped the talking, the looking, the asking,
the learning, the doing.
I created space to let things be.
I heard my heartbeat.
I felt its pulse.
I experienced sensations of life alive within me.
I felt into the sensations.
I rode them like a skilled surfer on a wave.
I explored the caverns in the body.
I discovered wisdom waiting to be received.
I touched the center of the wounds and loved them into wholeness.
I rescued the pieces of me lost inside in a time long ago.
I sat with all parts of me getting to know them,
understand them, nurture them, love them.
I saw my light.
I followed it into the recesses of my heart.
I found what I thought I was missing.
A golden brilliance of light tucked away deep inside, perfectly
tended to, and cared for, waiting for me to come home.

It was the last place I looked, and the only place
where it was always safe.
It was my own light, my own love.
I learned how to embody it, to be with it, to care
for it, and to use it.
The light in the heart is the lighthouse of the soul;
May you always follow this light and let it guide you home.

~Kate Shipp~

EPILOGUE

As I sit here writing this to you, it is the end of 2021. The past two years have been a time of great overwhelm, despair, and fear for so many in this world. COVID-19 affected all lives in many different ways. I often pray in gratitude to have worked through the trauma before the pandemic hit the world. My ability to navigate trauma helped me in being present to the many emotions vacillating through my system during these trying times. I have also been blessed with helping many others learn how to do the same. The constant wondering early on of when it would end, leading to the transition away from the world as we knew it, to the still yet-to-be-discovered world that will be.

The timeline of this first book ends in 2018. There is much more to share on how God taught me how to use the breath as a form of therapy not just a practice; how God showed me the Divine Feminine as a way of love; how my marriage navigated through this time of tragedy into a time of great love and intimacy that I never thought I could experience because we both did our own work individually and together; how my children went through their own trauma healing with incredible therapists and naturopathic care; how my kids and I healed our attachment wounds and did deep repair work to overcome the ways my trauma caused them pain.

This story doesn't cover the many moments where I conversed with Spirit about how to serve in this world, the many practices

I used to help support myself between therapy sessions, and my favorite go-to practices and processes for continued self-therapy and post-traumatic growth. There will be much more shared as I am called to write more and teach this connection to the Love that lives alive in you seeking you always.

I was in weekly trauma therapy for almost five years, from 2016 through 2020. In January 2020, I started seeing another therapist as Darla had moved out of state (I did see her remotely for a while but wanted to continue in-person sessions). My new therapist is excellent and helped me to understand that I had missed a critical step in my recovery, that being the right placement of responsibility for my safety, protection, and emotional holding. I did another year of weekly therapy to reprogram how my body was still holding responsibility for the emotional pain of others, and gave back responsibility for my own protection and care when I was little. I still go to therapy as needed.

This therapist inspired me to study Internal Family Systems work[11]. According to the Internal Family Systems Institute, "Internal Family Systems is a powerfully transformative, evidence-based model of psychotherapy. We believe the mind is naturally multiple and that is a good thing. Our inner parts contain valuable qualities and our core Self knows how to heal, allowing us to become integrated and whole." [12]

This deeper understanding of how the parts of our psyche actually present in different parts of our body, and cause symptoms of distress to get our attention, helped me to understand how while I was living life in a beautiful way, I was also still trying to dodge parts of myself seeking my love. The journey this past year has been joyful and enlightening as I continue to learn how to love all parts of me, and show up in this world in my wholeness each day.

Starting in 2016, I was in weekly acupuncture for six months, then bi-weekly for six more months, then monthly for a year, and still as needed. I see a different naturopath regularly. When I review all the modalities and methods that helped me overcome CPTSD as a daily struggle, there were over thirty offerings. This is what that means to me: find what works for you and stick with it. When it stops working, there will be other tools brought into your life to help you on this journey.

The journey of recovery has no timeline and there is no full ending. I believe we are always learning how to navigate being human with more grace and ease. It is my hope that as we come through these hard times we will be a human species with more compassion, more acceptance, more understanding, more generosity, and more love. I pray that in the moments when you are suffering and don't know how you can go on any further, you take three deep breaths and connect to your heart. I pray that you find the sensations in your feet and notice your connection to the Earth. I pray that you seek to understand and know the Divine being that you are, sent here on this very special place for a very intentional purpose. I pray that you are gentle and kind to yourself, and you begin to walk a journey of self-love with the right support and safe people at your side. I pray you find your connection to Spirit, if you don't have it already, and devote time each day to become deeply intimate with this light that you are.

There is gold being forged in the fire. As uncomfortable as it can be to let it burn, a powerful Phoenix is rising deep inside of you. You are worthy of living a life you love. I pray that when you wake up each day you are able to say, "I'm clocking in, God. Let's do this. May they encounter your love today when they interact with me."

"...And I pray that He would unveil within you the unlimited riches of His glory and favor until supernatural strength floods your innermost being with His divine might and explosive power.

[17] *Then, by constantly using your faith, the life of Christ will be released deep inside you, and the resting place of His love will become the very source and root of your life.*

[18-19] *Then you will be empowered to discover what every holy one experiences — the great magnitude of the astonishing love of Christ in all its dimensions. How deeply intimate and far-reaching is His love! How enduring and inclusive it is! Endless love beyond measurement that transcends our understanding — this extravagant love pours into you until you are filled to overflowing with the fullness of God!*

[20] *Never doubt God's mighty power to work in you and accomplish all this. He will achieve infinitely more than your greatest request, your most unbelievable dream, and exceed your wildest imagination! He will outdo them all, for his miraculous power constantly energizes you."* (Ephesians 16-20, TPT.)

SUPPLEMENTAL STORY

My dad was diagnosed with acute myeloid leukemia on November 25, 2022. He had gone to the hospital on November 21 to have his heart checked due to shortness of breath and a couple of other symptoms. Many tests and four days later, we got the life-altering news. The next fifty-five days would be an experience I never thought I would go through and a journey no one can prepare you for. For those seven weeks I traveled back and forth to Chicago, helping Dad and supporting the rest of my family, as we all walked this together. My hand was on my dad's heart, feeling its slowing rhythm as he took his final breath at 1:33 a.m. on January 14, 2023 – my forty-second birthday.

The following chapters are his, and were meant to form the beginning of his second book. I think he started them in 2014 or 2015, and I'd always hoped he would write more, but he remained stuck for many years. He shared these chapters with me in the summer of 2021, as the final draft of my own book was close to being complete, and kindly offered for me to include them. After lengthy discussions with him, I told him to keep them and finish his book. It is his story of what happened the night I died twice, and it was his alone to tell.

Dad mentioned my death three times to me during my trips to Chicago between November 2022 and January 2023. He mentioned it the first time at the end of November when he was at Northwestern Hospital awaiting his cancer treatment. He said he couldn't listen to meditations with my voice because all he saw when he heard my voice was me lying dead in the hospital.

On the night of December 28, when I was staying at the hospital with him, I sat in his bed holding his hand. He started crying and said, "Katie, I watched you die twice."

We spent the next hour talking about how I'm okay now, I'm alive and well, and I will be okay. Still crying, he said how he would sometimes see me dying when he closed his eyes. He told me through his tears that he was so sorry and should have been there for me more as a child and teen. He and I went through some deep healing over the years I was in trauma therapy, as I held a lot of guilt and shame over this event. Our relationship from 2016 to 2023 had never been closer.

He made me promise I would be okay if he died, and he went through each one of my family members, saying whether or not he thought they would be okay. He said he wanted to know his family would be okay without him here. It was during that conversation that I told him he didn't owe us anything and to fight if he wanted to fight, and that he'd done well to change the family legacy he inherited. It was a conversation I will remember for the rest of my life.

A couple of days before his death, he was barely opening his eyes and not communicating much through words, although he tried. After he brought up the event a third time to me and once to my sister, Suzy, I told him I would add these chapters to my book and name him as their author. I told him that his story of this event needed to be shared and that it would hopefully give his soul some closure to what he went through that night. When I shared this with him, his eyes opened and he had tears. He nodded.

It's not an easy read. I have a very different relationship with this experience from my past now. It is a beautiful one, one of immense gratitude and understanding of how this event changed the trajectory of my life.

Dad is very present with me in different ways now. It will never be the same and I am navigating the full human journey of grief with compassion and love as I connect to his Spirit throughout the day. I hope you enjoy the voice of my dad and his loving Spirit in these words.

VISION OF EAGLE/STRENGTH OF BEAR

BOOK II

By Allan Lombardo, EagleBear

Part One

In Which World Do You Live?

I NEED YOUR HELP

by

Allan Lombardo

It was a typical late Sunday afternoon in mid-December. I was watching the local Arizona news on television while my wife, Kathy, was preparing dinner for the three of us. My youngest daughter, Mickey Pat, was finishing her math homework. Then the wall phone in the kitchen rang.

"Hello, this is Kathy." She was stretching the extra-long coiled phone cord across the kitchen, balancing it between her ear and shoulder as she tried to turn over the searing meat braising in a pan on the stove. "I'm sorry, doctor, would please say that again?" Next, I heard the phone's handset crack as it hit the tile floor, and her yelling to me in the adjoining great room: "Oh my God! Allan!"

We had not spoken to our daughter, Kate, who was a freshman at ASU in Tempe, for a few days – not unusual during weekdays. However, we, especially her mom, always heard from her over the weekends. I assumed that she was still upset with me after our heated discussion last Sunday about her boyfriend. The more I tried to alert her to his poor choices in this life and his caustic brazen personality in not dealing with them, the more she defended his behavior. How many times did she have to remind us that Trask came from a broken family and was raised in several foster homes? Since she was a little girl, Kate was always finding the strays of society, determined that she could make their lives better – or at least less pain-filled with some one-on-one attention and a dose of humorous laughter.

Over the past year her latest rescue project, Trask, had joined the Marines; however, within only a few months of her boyfriend's enlistment, he intentionally managed to get himself to be released from his military service – once again choosing another of many wrong paths in his young life because "it was too hard for him." Kate defended this dubious lack-of-character of a man by explaining that it was a mutual decision and not that it was just Trask's fault for being discharged (kicked out) by the Corps.

Having served in both the Navy and also assigned for a while with the Marines during the Vietnam War, I had a very good understanding of life in the military and the required learned discipline of taking and giving orders. My judgment in this matter was that Trask consciously screwed up, and so badly that he got his ass booted out of the service. This immature man's alleged ancestry aggravated me even more after he boasted that his great-grandfather was Comanche Jack Stillwell who "killed those damn Redskins" when he rode with General George Custer. He bragged that he was responsible for killing the Cheyennes' great chief, Roman Nose, but after searching through historical records this could never be verified. My daughter used the excuse that Trask acted the way he did because he had a dysfunctional family. I retorted, "It's obvious that it runs in all of his ancestors' genes – and not just in their pants."

"Allan, Kate's in the emergency room! The doctor said it's serious and we need to get there NOW!" My wife was hurriedly putting the meat in the refrigerator, taking off her apron, and grabbing her purse. Within seconds she was already waiting for me at the door leading to the garage. "Mick, you better come with us. Better bring any unfinished homework...may be at the hospital for a while..."

"Mom, what happened to Kate? Did she get hurt? Is she bleeding?" Mickey Pat kept machine-gunning questions, making us even more nervous than the initial shock of learning Kate was in an emergency room and not knowing why.

As I backed the car out of the driveway, I looked at Kathy who was sobbing in the passenger seat. "Honey, what else did the doctor tell you? Was Kate in an accident...in her VW? Is she conscious?" I could sense that she knew more but was trying to keep it to herself.

"He said that she is unconscious..." Kathy whispered, sniffling "...he did not think she had much time...Where was she? Who was she with? Why didn't someone call us sooner?"

Mickey was starting to cry in the back seat of our Jeep.

"Not much time, what the hell does that mean? If that idiot boyfriend of hers had anything to do with this, I'll kill him!" My anger was getting the better of me – even if justified. "Where the hell is this damn hospital located? How do I get there? Are you sure Clark gave you the right directions?" Kathy tried to compose herself as she repeated his driving directions to the John C. Lincoln Hospital.

I wanted to drive through as many red lights as possible, but controlled my emotional urge, not wanting to end up in an accident – no need for us to end up like Kate. I was assuming that she had been in a car crash. This wouldn't be the first time she allowed her numb-nuts boyfriend to drive her Rabbit convertible. How many times had I told her that our State Farm policy only covers family members? – and that this jerk was never going to be part of this family if I had anything to say about it.

"Dad, are we almost there?"

Looking in the rear-view mirror I could see that Mickey Pat was really upset. Kate was her only sibling living with her in Arizona. Her other sister, Jewels Anne, was finishing college in Ann Arbor at the University of Michigan. Her two brothers, already graduated from college, were working professionals in the Chicago and Indianapolis metropolitan areas. Thinking of my out-of-state children triggered even more panic – we hadn't called to alert them of Kate being in the hospital. I tried to calm myself by telling myself that it was best to wait. My kids would have too many questions about their sister and I didn't have the answers for them at this time.

"We are only about a mile away, Mick. Keep praying that your sister will be okay." Kathy was very nervous. She had her rosary wrapped around her fingers. "Allan, take that entrance to the emergency room...parking is over there...hurry..." After parking we ran to the ER entrance doors. Little did I know that I needed to prepare myself for the worst and the ultimate pain that a parent should never have to experience – the death of his child.

Doctor Lei Xiong was waiting for us at the inner doors to the ER. His facial expression confirmed my greatest fear. We hastily introduced ourselves as he led us into the ER treatment area. My ears heard him speaking, but my head was only catching words – tidbits – as my mind raced, creating visualizations of my daughter, Kate: Saturday night college party...drugs...Ecstasy...overdose...found her body...bathroom floor...police...ambulance...unconscious...pumped her stomach...charcoal ...And then I heard his somber words, "I'm so sorry...there is nothing more that we can do. She is in the Almighty's hands now." My mind was thinking that maybe it would have been better if she was in an auto accident.

"May we see her?" Tears were streaming down her face as Kathy squeezed my hand. I looked into her eyes, searching for an answer as to why this was happening. My wife's eyes only responded with sadness and bewilderment.

Dr. Xiong responded, "I think it best that only you and Allan see her right now." Kathy took Mickey Pat to the visitors' waiting room, trying to give her some encouragement that Kate would get through this and to keep praying for her sister.

As we entered the ER treatment bay, the doctor pushed the curtains aside. I saw a sallow motionless young female with a gray-black ash substance smeared on her front body parts lying on a slab-like bed. Her dark reddish-brown curly hair was disheveled and matted. An IV was in her wrist with numerous monitors connected, some beeping, as a nurse was watching over her lifeless form. I thought, *This can't be my Kate! My daughter is so lively and full of fire and love for life.* I let Kathy lead the way as we approached her ghostly stillness.

"Oh, Kate, my dear sweet Kate...What have you done to yourself this time?" Her mother touched her right hand, hoping to feel a response from her daughter. "Allan, her skin is so cold. Oh my God..."

There are no words that can describe such a moment of pain and sadness – such utter helplessness. I had recently reconciled within myself all the guilt, grief and related familial emotions that a child, a son, feels upon losing from this world not one, but both parents: his mother and his father dying within hours of one another in May of this year, 1999. My mystical role as the "Angel of Death" assisted me with preparing myself and them to experience a more peaceful crossing over to the other side. But now the tables were reversed. I needed to prepare myself, this time as the parent, for possibly losing one of his children, his second daughter, to some deadly "recreational" drug.

"Kathy, I won't allow it! I have seen Kate in my visions and she has a very long life ahead of her. This is not her time to leave us! Stay with her. I must call Clark and Connie-Mom and ask for their help."

She looked up at me with such tear-filled green eyes. "Don't let them take her, EagleBear. You keep our Kate here with us... our daughter...safe...in my arms. Now go and do what you have to do..."

As I left the ER waiting room, I was hoping that she did not notice my Grandpa Allan's Hopi ring, the Hopi-made silver one with thunderbirds and kachinas with a brown/black agate picture stone, buzzing on my right hand's ring finger – the same ring that I wore in the past when I summoned my departed grandfather to assist with both Kathy's parents and my parents' crossing over to the other side.

I returned to the waiting room, scanning the occupied chairs to see if Kate's boyfriend was hanging around. Mickey Pat came over to me asking if there was any change with Kate.

I shook my head. "Have you seen Trask?"

"Yes, Daddy, but he immediately left when he heard you were here. He wanted to know where you wanted him to drop off Kate's VW. He wouldn't tell me what happened to Kate. He looked really scared."

"Mick, it's a good thing he got his ass out of here...that piece of shit. I'll deal with him later...once we get your sister back...I mean when she's better. I need to make some calls. Please go back in the ER and stay with Mom and Kate. Get me if Kate's condition changes. Thanks, Mick."

I went outside, checked the battery level on my cellphone, and hit the letter "C." It rang twice. An unfamiliar, more serious voice answered. "Hello, EagleBear. Was last night's gathering too long? I didn't realize how late it was...was it past two a.m. when we finished?"

There was no time to respond with pleasantries. "Clark, I need your help! Kate...unconscious...not good...yes, doc says dying...see you in fifteen minutes. Thanks."

My next call was to Grandmother Elder WolfWoman, or "Connie-Mom." Before I could say hello, the ageless elder mystic answered, "EagleBear, I am so sorry about your daughter, Kate. I know...you need our help. We will do what we must do to bring her back – that is, if she wants to return to her body. Being with the Light can be very intoxicating. One's spirit usually wants to remain with the Life Source if it is her time. No...she is not done with her true purpose on this planet...much greater life-path to fulfill. This won't be easy. Ask Clark to contact the rest of our Table of Twelve. We'll need to work together. Let's gather in Hermes' sacred Emerald Tablets Room of the Ancient of Days. Be strong, EagleBear. See you there shortly."

"Thank you, Grandmother Elder WolfWoman. Peace and Blessings."

If anyone would be able to reclaim my daughter, she had that unexplainable mystic ability and power. And yet, even she acknowledged that it would take the combined forces of our inner circle and then some to keep Kate from crossing over to the other side.

I called my daughter, Jewels Anne, in Michigan. Kathy and I had spoken to her much earlier in the day wishing her a happy birthday – her twenty-first! Unfortunately, this conversation held a much more serious tone. After informing her of Kate's grave condition, I asked her to contact her brothers and stand by for any further news.

Jewels' initial response was," Kate doesn't do drugs, but her worthless boyfriend probably does. Trask's such a loser, Dad."

I told her that we would deal with Trask later. Jewels Anne wanted to catch a flight to Phoenix right away, but I emphasized that she needed to pass her semester final exams. After a few minutes of demonstrating her usual stubbornness, she agreed to stay up all night, if necessary, studying for her finals; she was no longer in the mood for celebrating her birthday anyway after learning about Kate. She would wait until after her final exams were taken and for our call that Kate was out of the woods before booking a flight to Phoenix. I wish I had Jewels' unwavering belief and confidence that our mystical healers would get her sister healed.

I was pacing outside waiting for Clark, the shaman, to arrive. I wondered if there were any changes in Kate's vitals. Suddenly I heard Mickey Pat shouting. "Daddy, Daddy where are you? WE NEED YOU!"

CHAPTER 2

DEATH'S REVOLVING DOOR

by
Allan Lombardo

I heard my youngest daughter's cry for help. I ran back inside to where Kate was being treated in the emergency room. Kathy and Mickey Pat were crying and standing in front of a pulled curtain. There were doctors and nurses behind that curtain with raised, nervous voices as I heard the flatline sound from the monitor, "Clear!", and the paddles sending electrical shocks to Kate's almost nineteen-year-old failing heart. The scene was surreal as the three of us jumped each time we heard the Asian voice warning "Clear!" The machine continued to utter the same piercing droning pitch. And then there was total silence. "Let the record show patient died at 7:19 p.m."

Clark came running into the emergency room as Dr. Xiong pushed the curtain aside, and said, "I'm so sorry to inform you..." The shaman's presence startled the doctor and I took the opportunity to interrupt.

"Doctor, time is of the essence. I don't have time to explain... except to tell you that we may be able to bring Kate back. Please allow our friend, Clark, a shaman, to use his good medicine on our daughter."

As the Chinese physician looked into Clark's dark black eyes, I detected an almost reverence of recognition for the Native American-trained medicine man. Dr. Xiong allowed Clark to treat Kate's departed body and soul. So many past times I have seen that familiar faraway, glazed look of his. I instinctively knew that Clark – as well as Grandmother Elder WolfWoman – had already been performing their mystical rituals on Kate as he was driving to the hospital.

Clark closed the curtain around my daughter's lifeless form and proceeded to utter those familiar guttural sounds of a chanting medicine man. There was no time for awkwardness with informing Dr. Xiong that we were involved with a group of psychics and mystic healers who have been practicing the ancient rituals of soul retrieval. If the doctor only knew the remarkable story about how we were able to retrieve the soul of the Chief of all Medicine Men, Thunder Bear, four years earlier in 1995.

"When I grew up in China, my grandmother taught me her skills and knowledge of treating illness with herbal remedies and Oriental medicine techniques. Believe me, it took me many years to truly understand how effective her old ways were and that Western medicine is only one of many ways to confront and alleviate illness and pain. Who am I to question the ways of mine or others' ancestors' healing modalities and rituals? But I must advise/confirm to you that your daughter has died." Dr. Xiong looked emotionally drained and exhausted.

Kathy and Mickey Pat were overcome with grief. Kate was gone...dead...and they were never to hear their second daughter's/her sister's laughter again.

"Doctor, could you please take them out to the waiting room, while I assist my friend? I'll come get you as soon as Kate...it is time."

He put his arms around them and walked them out.

As I looked through the curtain, I observed Clark sweeping Kate's lifeless body with an eagle's feather as he continued his chanting with a rattle in his left hand. I mentally called upon Thunder Bear, the Chief of all Medicine Men, to please intercede with our Great Father in the Sky and return my daughter to us. I also prayed to God, Jesus and his mother, Mary, begging to please bring my daughter back to us. I detected a buzzing on my ring finger. "Grandpa Allan, is that you? Can you help? Please, please bring my Kate back from the Light. It's not her time yet to join you and her grandmother, Virginia." As I stared at my daughter's "dead" body, I detected the slightest movement in her right hand. I took her hand and squeezed it, making contact with my grandfather's ring.

Then I heard a beep...another beep...and finally a continuous beep of the heart monitor machine. As I was staring back and forth between Clark and my daughter, her eyes opened. Dr. Xiang and a stream of nurses came rushing into that holy space where my daughter lay. "Please step aside..." spoke the Oriental doctor. Clark stepped back but kept staring through Kate's eyes. I left the doctor and his nurses attending to Kate. Clark and I found Kathy and Mickey Pat in the hospital's waiting room, anxious to give them the most welcome news.

"She's back! She's back! We – Clark – did it! We can't thank you enough!" Kathy and Mickey Pat were overcome with joy from the happy news and excitement as they hugged Clark and me. Such a joyous time!

"Oh, Kate, we're never ever going to let you out of our sight... ever!" Kathy exclaimed. "Can we see her?"

However, Clark was still in a daze and his eyes looked clouded. He appeared too mellow and somewhat out of it – kind of like being in the middle of a deep channel and trying to wake up from a dream that has not yet finished. The shaman began to mumble words so slowly "...Kate....not back...soul trapped...both worlds...needs more of us...help...time short... must try to save...Moses...Hermes..." The large unshaven man in black Bermuda shorts and a Chicago Bulls t-shirt stood up, wobbling trying to get his balance, as I grabbed his hulking frame and gently pushed him against the wall.

"Clark, what is it? What's wrong?"

He just stared at me with that same look as when a deer freezes when seeing an oncoming car's headlights. He tried to speak but could only mutter grunting sounds. Then I remembered my conversation with Connie-Mom.

"Clark, Grandmother Elder WolfWoman told me we will need the Table of Twelve to get Kate back." The medicine man nodded. "She said that we must meet in..." I was trying to remember the medicine woman's exact words "...Hermes' sacred Emerald Tablets Room of the Ancient of Days."

"Yes...must do...now!" Clark began to walk slowly toward Kate's ER treatment room. I motioned to my wife and daughter to stay in the visitors' waiting room. As we approached the double doors of the emergency room, Dr. Xiong came out with a smile on his face.

"Hi," he said softly. "Although Kate is still unconscious, your daughter is breathing on her own and her heart rate is stable. I could have sworn we lost her, but your friend – shaman – brought her back...saved her." Dr. Xiong looked into Clark's still murky eyes and said, "Thank you." The elated doctor then began to walk over to speak to my wife when suddenly the code blue warning blasted through the hospital's speakers.

Clark and I were still walking over to Kate's bedside when Dr. Xiong went running past us looking panic-stricken. The entire crash team was already hovering over Kate's lifeless form as we heard the sound of the flatlined monitor and someone yelling, "Step Back! Clear!" Those words kept resonating in my ears with that awful thump of a dying body rising/falling from the electric surge/shock. My mind was reeling with horrific thoughts of Kate's physical body being wracked with pain as her soul was pleading to release itself. How would she be able to survive another near-death experience?

We heard for the second time that evening the pronounce-ment of Kate's death. This time we almost did not recognize Dr. Xiong as he approached us, drenched in his own sweat and with such an overwhelming look of sadness. He attempted to utter some consoling words but his tear-filled eyes spoke for him. Almost instantly, Clark stood up perfectly straight, appearing as a giant towering over the despondent doctor, and placed a "bear-claw-like" hand upon his shoulder. "My friend, it is now time for Thunder Bear's medicine to retrieve Kate's soul...for she is about to decide/accept her chosen purpose in this life...her life-path as written in the Book of Life." Turning his head, the shaman then looked through me and spoke in that most familiar voice from the Multiverse, "Come, EagleBear. It's time for us to do what we have been trained to do – The Table of Twelve awaits our presence." As the medicine man/healer pulled the curtain closing the outside world from viewing my daughter's still body, the Western medi-cine team of doctors and nurses huddled, speaking in whispered voices in the emergency room.

I remember Clark taking my right hand, touching my grandfa-ther's Hopi ring, and extending it over my daughter's lifeless body. After instructing me to close my eyes and focus upon bringing my daughter back again – her soul was being even more attracted to the Light – the shaman then began to chant in his Native American guttural sounds while brushing over Kate with an eagle feather. Next, the medicine man shook his rattle over the perimeter of her body in a slow but ever-increasing rhythm. I found myself becom-ing mesmerized in the moment, feeling a shift within my body, and my mind falling into a dream-like state. I slowly drifted away into another dimension of time and space in the Multiverse...

CHAPTER 3

THE TABLE OF TWELVE

by
Allan Lombardo

The room was very long, almost tunnel-like, with shimmering green/azure blue walls reflecting the colors of the Northern Borealis. In the center of the sacred space was a massive round hand-hewn wooden table with twelve throne-shaped chairs evenly spaced. I could vaguely distinguish eleven human shapes occupying the room as I entered. As I glided past two massive metal doors which automatically locked shut, enclosing us in those secret chambers, I realized that I had entered Hermes' sacred Emerald Tablets Room of the Ancient of Days. Having good memories of visiting this room in past meditations, my inner self seemed to begin to calm itself as the brilliant, chakra-like colors reflecting off the walls of this hallowed space saturated my being.

I sat down in the remaining empty chair at one end of the table, focusing upon each of the other beings already seated. Clark was to my right, then, going counterclockwise, sat Thunder Bear, Chief Red Cloud, Chief Washakie, Sacagawea, Farley Day, Sondra Yeh, Debra Vines, Mary Fullove, and Grandmother Elder WolfWoman; to my left was a most beautiful Native American young woman. I acknowledged each healer and his/her special shamanistic gift of healing and thanked all members for attending this most special gathering. I then turned to my left and was about to ask the fair maiden her name when she took my left hand and squeezed it, her radiance now filling the room with the light of the Light.

"I am so deeply honored," I said, "that you have blessed our table with your presence, my Lady, Mary. Today you appear as White Buffalo Calf Maiden. At other times you have appeared at Lourdes, Fatima, Guadalupe...so many times to give us such important special messages for the Earth Mother and Her people. We need your guidance with our good intention to bring my daughter back into her body."

"EagleBear," she replied, "your daughter has been carrying much pain and torment within both her soul and body for many moons. These wounds are so deep and the memories so black that her Spirit seeks freedom from that embedded hurt. For the second time this day she has tasted the Light and wishes to remain at peace with Him. Nevertheless, the Ancient of Days, KEEPER OF SPIRIT, recognizes her own past written entry in her Book of LIFE stating that your daughter, Kate, chose this deadly trauma as her pathway to finding what her true purpose for her own life is and to use these life lessons for assisting others with healing within themselves. Should Kate still want to choose to live again – and ONLY she can make that choice by using her free will – then she must accept the conditions and consequences of returning into her physical body. Her journey will not be easy, will be filled with suffering at times, but also will be gifted with wonderful blessings."

She continued, "However, I caution you, EagleBear, should Kate accept her fate by returning to her body, she will begin to live her new life in a duality of consciousness. She, having lived among the living and now among the dead, this state of intellect will at times attract souls and spirits who have not fully crossed over from life to death – meaning that some beings feel they have unfinished business and that death robbed them of its completion, which puts them into a state of limbo searching endlessly to transition to the afterlife."

As she looked at each healer around the table Mary concluded with this directive: "You are all here together to assist Kate with whatever help she needs to choose either to cross over to the afterlife or to return to her physical body and continue her life's journey on the Red Road. May you guide her accordingly with choosing wisely – but SHE must make the final life/death choice." After much discussion, the consensus of this group of healers was that Kate must rebirth her soul and heal her own self by providing guidance and healing to others who are suffering from their own traumatic life experiences.

I opened my eyes, looking at my daughter's lifeless form and then observing Clark holding his pendulum over Kate's solar plexus, its amethyst stone spinning so fast that it created a cyclonic vibrational effect of motion. Suddenly, a hand grasped the purple healing gem, and as she clutched it, Kate's body rebirthed back to life for the third time. Tears began to roll down her cheeks and her flesh began to regain some of its vibrant color. Before I could react, doctors and nurses were rushing around her body with IVs, monitors, and a myriad of related medical activities as so many voices kept repeating words of shock and amazement. Dr. Xiong gave both Clark and me congratulatory hugs, continuing to stare at Kate and then the two of us, softly saying, "...such powerful Qi medicine...never seen anything like that...thank you..."

Clark and I never spoke and/or mentioned again about that special gathering of the Table of Twelve. It was a surreal encounter with both living and dead spirits who have influenced both of our lives as healers. A memory forever branded into our intellects and souls. When it is time, I will relate to my daughter, Kate, the magnificence of the occurrence under such life versus death consequences to her.

CHAPTER 4

DUALITY
OF CONSCIOUSNESS

by
Allan Lombardo

This is where he stopped writing. I find it so beautiful that these were his last authored words in his book.

More of his journey will be shared through the eyes and love of his family.

If you want to read more about my dad, you can look up his first book, *Vision of Eagle, Strength of Bear* by Allan Lombardo on Amazon.

ABOUT THE AUTHOR

Kate Shipp is a Christ-Centered yoga therapist, certified with the International Association of Yoga Therapy, and a 500ERYT and YACEP with Yoga Alliance. She holds a B.S. in Marketing from Arizona State University, and has thousands of hours in training and personal experience in various holistic therapies. For the past decade, Kate has specialized in seeing clients for mental health and trauma recovery. She uses the teachings of Jesus and the philosophy and practices of yoga, combined with the neuroscience of trauma, to help clients overcome painful pasts, remember their wholeness, and live lives of peace and joy.

Kate's personal recovery from Complex PTSD, and her connection to Spirit, motivate her to serve others in this way, and she believes that through hope, faith, and love even the most painful sufferings can be overcome.

Kate works with clients privately, online and in-person, as well as through group mentoring and various training programs. She is the creator of The Shipp Method™ of Christ-Centered Trauma Recovery, a training program to teach other therapeutic practitioners a seven-step process for Remembered Wholeness. Kate also offers various events, workshops, retreats, and presentations to educate, embody, and empower radiant living.

Kate is a bestselling author of two compilation books and a motivational speaker. Her work as a yoga therapist was featured in a documentary called, *The Box: Out of the Impossible,* about a woman's recovery from horrific trauma and abuse. She is a contributing author for Christian Yoga Magazine.

She resides in Phoenix, Arizona with her husband and two children. Two dogs and two cats complete her family. Kate loves being out in nature, and you will often find her with a cup of hot coffee in her hands.

STAY CONNECTED WITH KATE

You can connect with Kate online and via social media here:

Website: www.kateshipp.com - sign up for her email list!
facebook.com/kateshipp333
Instagram: kateshipp333
MightyNetworks: The Shipp Method Community

Kate regularly posts educational content to help support trauma recovery, mental health resources, and resilience. She also hosts events, workshops, mentoring offers, and trainings.

Her group mentoring program, The Shipp Method of Spiritually Embodied Living, is offered twice a year for six months. This program is a client favorite, offering a safe, loving community for the gentle processing of suffering while taking small steps forward in creating a life you love. Learn more at her website link, www.kateshipp.com/work-with-kate

Kate recently launched a community on MightyNetworks based on the 5 Truths of The Shipp Method: Safety, Compassion, Presence, Grace, Love. Join this community to have daily access to Kate's teachings and sharings without the ads, censoring, and distractions that are flooding other social media platforms. This is also where you will find her course offerings and be able to watch her live videos.

Be sure to download the free Safe Space Meditation offered at the beginning of the book. You can access this at www.kateshipp.com/shop.

As a bonus gift, at that same link, you can download the "Who God Says You Are" recording for free.

Be Well & Blessed.

ACKNOWLEDGMENTS

Thank you to my assistants for believing in this mission of creating a more compassionate, loving world through transformational practices for inner healing. Thank you to my publisher, Shanda Trofe, for your patience and encouragement as I birthed this book into the world. Thank you to my editor for your support and gift of voice.

Thank you to all of my teachers and mentors for pushing me just enough to take another step forward, for your compassion and grace, and for your continuous support and love. Thank you for seeing me when I couldn't see myself, and for not allowing me to settle for less than what I am capable of on this journey. Thank you for reminding me of the beauty of rest, and the need for stillness.

Thank you to my therapists and integrative medical team, who truly listen to me, collaborate with me, support me, and give me space to make decisions in a way that feels right for my healing.

Thank you to my clients for trusting me, for stepping boldly into your own healing, and for being willing to walk the way of love.

Thank you to my incredible circle of friends who inspire me, motivate me, encourage me, who love to play and have fun, and who are able to meet me in the worlds of humanity and spirit.

Thank you to Jeni and Marci, chosen sisters for decades now, who never gave up on me, who have always seen my authentic me, for showing me my blind spots in a gentle way, for helping me to see my greatness, for loving me through the hardest moments of pain, and for celebrating with me in the joys of success.

Thank you to the Shipp family for welcoming me with open arms 21 years ago, for embracing me for who I am, and for showing me how much crazy fun a family can enjoy together.

Thank you to my parents, who both were willing to hear the hard stuff, take responsibility for their part in it, for doing some of their own healing work, for forgiving me the pain I caused them, and for showing great love as I navigated very rough waters along the way.

Thank you to my siblings, who have always loved me for me, for the many moments of laughter and fun, and for reminding me of the good times when the pain clouded my memories.

Thank you to Connor and Makena, for showing me the meaning of love, for being my greatest mirrors and teachers, for believing in me, and for the willingness to do hard work at such a young age to heal and grow together as a beautiful family.

Thank you to my beloved, Eric, for being the embodiment of love, my rock of support, for believing in me, for being the greatest dad to our children, and for being so brave and courageous to do the deep work so we can live this life in joy as God intended it to be.

May the glory be God's, and may the Goodness of Love flow through all who read this book.

ENDNOTES

1. https://www.emdr.com/what-is-emdr/

2. Walker, Pete. (2013). COMPLEX PTSD: *From Surviving to Thriving: A Guide and Map for Recovering from Childhood Trauma.* CreateSpace Independent Publishing Platform.

3. Desikachar, T.K.V. (1995). *The Heart of Yoga: Developing a Personal Practice.* Rochester, VT: Inner Traditions International.

4. Porges, Stephen W. (2017). *The Pocket Guide to THE POLYVAGAL THEORY: The Transformative Power of Feeling Safe.* W. W. Norton & Company, Inc.

5. Desai, Kamini, PhD. (2017). YOGA NIDRA: *The Art of Transformational Sleep.* First Lotus Press,

6. https://eft.mercola.com/

7. Levine, Peter A. (1997). *Waking the Tiger: Healing Trauma: The Innate Capacity to Transform Overwhelming Experiences.*North Atlantic.

8. Taylor, Jill Bolte. *My Stroke of Insight: A Brain Scientist's Personal Journey.* (2009). Penguin Books.

9. Easwaran, Eknath. *The Upanishads.* (1987, 2007). Nilgiri Press.

10. Anodea, Judith. (2004). *Eastern Body, Western Mind: Psychology and the Chakra System as a Path to the Self.* Celestial Arts.

11. http://stephenbarnett.blogspot.com/2019/11/illuminate-eyes-ephesians-118-tpt.html

12. https://ifs-institute.com/

www.ingramcontent.com/pod-product-compliance
Lightning Source LLC
Chambersburg PA
CBHW071151130626
46553CB00004B/1603